BACK TO NIRVANA

BACK TO NIRVANA

DHARMA DIARY POEMS

VOLUME III

by

JOY MAGEZIS

BLACK
APOLLO
PRESS

First published in Great Britain by Black Apollo Press, 2018
Copyright © Joy Magezis
The moral right of the author has been asserted.
A CIP catalogue record of this book is available at the
British Library.
ISBN: 9781900355896

Cover by Kevin Biderman

To Bob
my life love
making this possible
You'll always be with me

CONTENTS

25 January 2012

Stabilising insights
through repetition
Each time afresh
Seen in new ways

The sculpture again
from different angles
Allows comprehension
of the whole piece

Beyond illusion
of somewhere to get to
Opening, deepening
in standing still

May I be willing
to let go of ego
with nothing to prove
I don't need to grasp

Shame, fear, guilt
traps of the mind
Smiling to these seeds
I am so much more

Moved here or there
what is the difference
In Oneness of whole
all the same place

How would I know
my want is best
Beyond clouded vision
great clarity of love

I can only walk
path for myself
in expanding forgiveness
Compassionate detachment

26 January 2012

Courage to publish
my poems as they are
exposing my weaknesses
along with the strengths

Courage to share
what I have learnt
though it lays bare
my deepest inner life

Courage to read
what I have written
beyond expectations
to edit and cut

Courage to allow
This zygote to grow
forming within
Coalescing toward birth

Courage past control
of what poems are
Merely facilitating
their formation into life

13 February 2012

Writing privilege
just what I want
Words flow from med
No one breathing, typing

Beyond editing analysis
back to this luxury
Whatever appears
that's what comes out

I let go to softness
hurt passes through
Such minor distraction
when in proportion

Snow still on ground
grandchildren enjoyed
Ella staying, Sophie joining
Kev, Helena art working

Kev finishes film
of left, peace bookshop
Grandparents met in one
Housman culture shines

Helena women's art
in post peace Irish
North, South, London
together in performance

Sleepless Ella's opened
to seeing scared's a feeling
Hugging her fear
it passes like a cloud

On second bedtime
wants led meditation
practiced in school
I combine with breathing

Ella's more relaxed
does drift off easier
Yes, she can touch
warm soft feeling

Sophie on Saturday
Big cousin and friend
Girls do puppet show
Play so well together

Bob and my seeds
continue, intermeshed
Trusting our union
Accepting life's flavours

So proud of Sophie
spirit so strong
Says I'm calm, smile
that Ali's kind

Sophie e-mails me
Valentines card
'Do anything for you'
So touched I reply

Kerin still ill
on antibiotics
Stephanie nursing
I send her thanks

Bob off to London
on coffee consultancy
After Reiki teaching
space alone for me

Room to see poems anew
resonate this life force
into word creations
Writing privilege

8 March 2012

Roots from women beaten
marching into posh district
Demanding basic rights
Care for people above money

Same values as Occupy
so many years before
Money seen as men's work
Helping people as women's

Occupy clustered
into Finsbury Square
After other evictions
sites joined as one

Those with greatest needs
have pitched their tents
Homeless woman poet
says living on grace

Friends from St Paul's
moving to small block
Car park below
mud, music above

People settling in
Getting to know each other
Wanting to make it work
Coming into new phase

Dream of eco-village
cheap sustainable builds
Model for homeless
of how to survive

Geodesic dome
Small wood dwelling
Newspaper construction
coming along soon

Cabaret tomorrow
from School of Ideas
Square's welcoming role
for events relocated

Working on many levels
Reminiscent of Women's Lib
The Personal is Political
Need to see misperceptions

Brother raps of brainwashing
in society ripe for change
I ask for men's support
to look at view of women

We all want the same
caring way of life
Occupy goals connect
International Women's Day

Barcelona Power
to walk and see
Miro inspires
creativity

In midst of Franco
he still finds ways
to express life clarity
unity and essence

Back to the land
where he grew up
Picasso chooses
the exile route

An ex-pat like him
I take on new place
Yet in my blood
universal Jew

Surprised at my stamina
to walk so far with Bob
Feet rise aliveness
in sand, rippling waves

Being both Gaudi city
and long, wide seaside
Sun's warmth revives
Art stimulates

Bob and I together
celebrating birthdays
Our new books born
The depth of our love

Another adventure
in sweet Catalonia
California of Spain
Barcelona Power

25 March 2012

Sixty-fifth party
such strong connections
Warmth spread round
Poems born to life

Bob made it happen
producing book, food
My dear life partner
Sweet family surround

Friends of old
Women's Lib
Sangha, kids
Neighbours join

Intermingling
Energy so good
Reading to them
in oral tradition

Heart flower cover
joint Kev, my design
Glowing out yellow
Pink pedals bloom

Book so Wabi Sabi
uniquely imperfect
Doing it our way
Family press

Comfortable with poems
after so many drafts
Page layouts different
Bob brings together

Just how I wanted
to turn sixty-five
with community
Love and light

From and into
this, my world
book naturally shines
Resonating

Lace, ice crystals
tears and warmth
reformed into words
created anew

Satisfied, satiated
Really there at party
Present with life flow
built to new chapter

This special time
Limited edition
Nothing to wait for
Future built on Now

27 March 2012

Shifting perspective
returning to stasis
Fear crept back
without my notice

Fresh walk on Green
after restless sleep
Responsaholic dreams
I see you old friends

As feet touch earth
in morning light
vividness grows
Trees become 3D

River stilled to lake
willows touch grace
Couple in canoe
lulled to this instant

Houseboat friends emerge
child and racy dogs
Thankful for warmth
after cold winter

Little Dolly smiles
happy sucking beads
Dad says stressed
so much work to do

Then we agree
that's how life goes
Expectations unreal
kids bring us back

Receiving the Now
Birds serenade
My dear fear
this is for you

30 March 2012   11 April 2012

Thich Nhat Hanh speaks in London then I attend his retreat

Royal Festival Hall
sold out to hear Thay
After led Meditation
he joins us with ease

Speaking of happiness
made of other elements
Suffering as part
Mud to grow lotus

Eyes of compassion
way to help loved-ones
When able to listen
such relief for them

Chanting to Avalokita
first for our own pain
Energy for loved-ones
then all of us, earth

As monastics sing
music so sweet
Opening begins
Audience stills

Transformation
process starts
So happy to accept
this harmony of love

In full auditorium
we resonate together
Energy immense
I touch my own pain

Heart widens
Out-breath release
Feeling surround
being with us all

Thay glowing
with such wisdom
Energy so wide
encompassing us all

Deep chewing
walking, hearing
speaking, singing
Resonating together

Precious sharing
of being alive
Touching Earth
as one organism

Leading by example
Teaching inner Buddha
Heart transmission
Thay's glow spreads

13 April 2012

24 April 2012

Embracing hiding fear with such tender love after Phung's releasing acupuncture treatment

Seeing in deep heart corner
old plague of worry wrath
Bringing badness upon us
mirroring badness within

Dharma rain
dropping into river
Instantly becoming
whole river at once

Find The Worst disaster
that could soon happen
Faith so hard to muster
Born right after holocaust

From the source
down to the sea
Past, present, future
Time disappears

Yet such love within
warmth of family hugs
Naches for us all
We survived and grow

Joy meditating
Thay within
Suddenly being
whole Sangha at once

Transforming to Joy
all that terror, horror
As Mom, Dad intended
in giving me my name

Commitment to positive
just as Thay says
Training ourselves
True wonderful thinking

With mind/heart clearing
easier to see old fear
crouching in darkness
manifesting confusion

Transforming for ancestors
precious decedents
Constructive catches up
neutralises old negative

Heaviness so intense
Shocked when I noticed
Worry seems entwined
in my very being

Star Trek feel
something bigger
Other worlds
right here within

Dear friend I understand
send non-blame acceptance
to you and my daughter
shifting vision to love

I can do it
drop by drop
Water warmth
embraces undermining

I offer you Now healing
fresh bloom of spring
Leaves bursting forth
recycling fear energy

21 April 2012

Preparing for family
birthday party for Sophie and Kerin

Awakened this morning
to discover Bob's presence
so alive and touchable
Here together for family day

This is our time
as parents had theirs
They enjoy through us
children/grand gathering

So blessed in this body
healthy to manifest
appreciate birth giving
so many years before

Surreal to imagine
adults from my uterus
such hope, tender babies
now share their own

We are the lineage
alive in us all
Fannie and Ed
Mom and Dad

May we enjoy
sweetness of harmony
Alive here together
Awakened this day

25 April 2012– 12 May 2012

GLIMPSES OF SPRING AWARENESS

You shock me
and I stop
Crimson so vivid
Blossom so fresh

Surprised I stare
Cannot move
Just here with you
again this spring

Looking and seeing
in three dimensions
You colour the world
being so alive

*   *   *

Bird sits on branch
I sit on stool
together just breathe
on cool spring day

You groom your feathers
I groom my mind
Free in this moment
of nothing but now

*   *   *

Pink blossom petals
scattered on cow dung
Wind washes through
earth link with foot

*   *   *

Being Bodhisattva
I already am
As leaf falls
I come back

Work accomplished
a thousand times over
No need to try
when already done

Surpassing tangles
from great ease
Being Bodhisattva
I already am

21 May 2012

I wrote these poems for artists at WYSING Arts Centre, as part of a workshop I did for them on Mindfulness and Reiki, including Reiki treatments.

ONLY ALIVE NOW

Body alive right here
Mind mostly elsewhere
in draw of the past
Planning for future

But we are only alive
in this split second
Past already gone
future hasn't happened

Connecting with breath
returns us to the now
Thoughts will distract
good to notice, come back

In beauty of stillness
oh, so vivid the trees
Clarity penetrating
earth's growth for us

Leaves' life-giving oxygen
replenishes out-breath again
Aware, taking in your gift
wakes us up to this instant

With mind, body together
energy streams through
Back into creative zone
where art manifests with muse

I am so very grateful
feet touching mother earth
Solid on our source planet
resonating such power

Reiki is this life force
blooming out foliage
Interchanging through us
Flowing interconnections

Illusion I stand along
surviving as separate self
when I'd die in a minute
without this treasured air

Being with this in-breath
just such a natural way
to harmonise my mind
with body alive right here

*EARTH WALKING
MIRACLE*

Mother Earth
I return to you
Unconditional love
linked through my feet

Great sustainer
I feel your pulse
vibrating in me
Me within you

Beyond dream walking
in fear's confusion
Clarity returns
touching you deeply

EXPLAINING REIKI

What is Reiki
that life force
turning bare trees
green with leaf again

All around
within/without
Spring sap rises
with vibration

We may not notice
so busy with projects
But out in nature
connection can be felt

Beauty bursting forth
in flower, sunset
Stopping to take it in
Expressing through art

Being in the zone
resonating with muse
Suddenly so vivid
Truly alive

Spiritual energy
of mother earth
nurturing healing
available in presence

EXPERIENCING

What is Reiki
this nurturing energy
Spiritually guided
washing out obstructions

I feel it through me
Tingling waves
Energy vibrations
cleansing old habits

Seeds remain
generations old
Picking weed shoots
Transforming compost

Intending compassion
Watching fear distraction
Just for today, now
do not worry, anger

Life practice
Awareness growing
River flowing timeless
All interconnected

No distinction
Reiki within/without
Opening to abundance
allowing healing through

Trusting process
Being Reiki flow
Ripples spreading
spiritual energy

1 – 22 June 2012

TWENTY-ONE DAY PLUM VILLAGE RETREAT

Three weeks to soften habits
Nurturing new ones to bloom
as lotuses burst forth
Freshness of life again

Walking in rain with Thay
Chopping veg with family
Sleeping upon earth
in tent connection

What a special time
I do want to share
Loosening delusion's grip
that somehow I'm separate

How reassuring to be
in planet organism
Forcefield felt
Simply whole

Coming back to sense
from marrow of being
that life is beauty flow
and I'm in vibration

Much easier this way
releasing defensive ego
Feeling safety in unity
Oneness to feed growth

*   *   *

Beautiful view from here
Thay says on veranda
Looking out with his eyes
Energy streams through

Greenness of trees
softly swaying love
Being in clear mind
happiness is seeing

Sunrise through Poplars
Sunset above pond
Bell strikes at dusk
Nun sings to heavens

Sun streaks pierce
whiteness of clouds
warming this body
Person called 'Joy'

Collection of past
experiences, actions
Non-Joy elements
networking now

Cooperating neurons
showing the way
Working together
with no controller

So much easier
just letting go
Eating breakfast
gift of mum

*   *   *

Such insights Thay shares
The obstacle of self
No thinking the secret
to step into Ultimate

Time circular not flat
allowing past back round
to be healed so well
As future built of now

Life time opportunity
to transform mistakes
Even before birth
deeply held guilt

All released in knowing
skilfulness can catch up
with negative actions
Change them at once

Confidence to trust
Store transforming
Patience for practice
No time, no hurry

Kindness to hurt
Feeding good seeds
Clarity, acceptance
of misperceptions

Resting in Sangha
Plum Village, UK
within this person
all creatures of earth

Feet link to you
Planet so alive
Yes, consciousness
dear mother radiates

In seeing true nature
purity all round
Connection with difficult
Ease of love below

Planting lotus seeds
in mud of judging, fear
Making good use
of compost noticed

Relaxed in knowing
no self to suffer
Clarity in being
this very action

Subject, object together
both underpinned
by ground of Ultimate
All intertwined

In tent lightening storm
safest place to dwell
is calm of Nirvana
True home of Now

Nourishing, nourishing
heart expansion
Lucid mind watches
lotus seed sprout

1 July – 17 July 2012

SUMMER GLIMPSES

Dog, cats and cows
River stillness calm
Birds serenading
as I stroll through

Stepping round
loose pooh patties
No need to be stuck
in discrimination

Letting go, letting go
Attachment release
for summer expansion
wide into bloom

Misperceptions
Responsaholic
Using wisdom sword
to cut the cord

Feathers float by
gliding on air
Ease of non-grip
best for us all

Loved-one separate person
though we're all connected
Intelligent compassionate
detachment frees us both

*   *   *

Sun shining
moon rising
on two sides of
very same sky

Me in-between
gently strolling
as cows munch
on the Green

*   *   *

Cosmos within
Each part of whole
White light clarity
All spectrum colours

Everyone unique
Colours combine
in different mixtures
Some purple or green

So many shades
bringing delight
Beyond dark cover
shining bright Oneness

*   *   *

Dropping lotus seeds
on darkest manure
When clearly seen
it's so very useful

Acceptance, acceptance
of my mind muck
No longer judged
seeds can sprout wide

Within Oneness
lotuses grow up
out of dank mud
once thought impure

29

30 July – 2 August 2012

TALKING INTERBEING WITH SIX YEAR OLD ELLA

Yes, she knows trees
give us oxygen
They use out-breath
We help each other

So easily she sees
how we drink cloud
Yes, we need water
How thirsty we'd be

Daddy told her story
how milk goes round
From cows to her
and then back again

And that light source
round ball in sky
The sun, of course
We need that star

Without it cold, dark
We have to have it
Couldn't see food
or even toys to play

Maybe that tree
that gives us apples
Is our great, great, great
great, great grandma

We both agree
all these make us
And she knows genes
You told me already

Finishing her fruit
deposited round face
'I've got an idea
You could make this
into a meditation'

*　　　*　　　*

Into new dimension
Ella able to read
Puppets, poems, songs
own points of view

Supporting her parents
a part of family life
East End community
New generations

We talk of Kev's essay
His face glows bright
Academia empowering
his thoughts, creativity

Helena off to Dublin
North/South women perform
Together across borders
building Irish bonds

*　　　*　　　*

Ella for the week
spunky, creative
messy, exhausting
Oh, so heart-warming

Sharing lives
Making jokes
Focusing attention
on this bright person

Strength of feeling
teaching, learning
remembering, renewing
love's continuation

10 August 2012

SAVOURING SOPHIE

Sophie new level
Banter and books
She reads so focused
and jokes own way

So at home with us
her projects with Bob
Raspberry Pi
Our cycle rides

Happy to have her
with such ease
Visiting Kerin
Their day tomorrow

And now tonight
after reading in bed
she asks for a hug
we both so enjoy

12 August 2012

Practicing Transformation
with dear Sophie
Tired on the way back
from long family bike ride

Wanting to stop and read
new book Bob bought her
She picked one on wizardry
talking of transformation

I say I'm good at that
she asks what it is
Changing one thing to another
She reads and I meditate

When I let go of hurry
need to get back home
river is so wondrous
Ducks and boats glide by

I could sit for lifetimes
on bank with granddaughter
My parents happily join us
Enjoying beauty together

Though her legs had hurt
after she reads and rests
Sophie says let's bike on
We cycle to the next bench

Here I did sketch for Mom
when she was ill in hospital
Sharing, we talk and laugh
Mood in full swing

Tired, Sophie makes it back
We'll try to fix bike gears
Now I savour our journey
Practicing Transformation

5 - 14 August 2012

Feeling inner tenderness
reacting deep within
to 'freeloader' word
Touching soft spot

Society's values
so easily transmitted
Working class freeloaders
but banker bonus natural

From childhood eyes
we all have feelings
Perhaps if not so branded
don't know what it's like

So easy to slip into
dualistic mindset
Defensive or judging
seen as only choices

I see this within me
coming out fighting
for what seen as unjust
arising from deep hurt

Moving beyond
knowing what it's like
to be 'common girl'
with so much to prove

We each have own hurts
various types of bullying
Misperceptions put upon us
causing such dark pain

Practicing together
we share great desire
to transform us, others
into true-self beings

In this process
of great awakening
soft spots within
are loved in the light

*   *   *

Into store base
of ancient infection
Grinding away
generations long

Undermining
present best efforts
with self-defeating
loathing of me

So glad I noticed
can make good use
New layer discovered
while mining in depths

*   *   *

Attentive loving
to wiggly part
Ego, brain bit
which entices
to pull back

Yes, I understand
that fear's in the way
But when you let go
such beauty appears
tenderly embracing

Kindly watching
Catching earlier
Allowing energy
beyond fight
to hold and wash

26 August 2012

FAMILY RETREAT AT NEW BARN 2012

Kerin sings
Sophie lightens
I savour
family bond

Childhood peace
chaos and order
in family practice
through play and being

From tiny to teen
each participates
Puppets and paints
Pottery and song

Building mindful habits
to eat, walk, breathe
'Everyone's nice'
granddaughter says

Sophie the hero
having good time
So her own person
Has always been

Listening, speaking
practice new for some
Learning fresh ways
to resolve conflict

Working out
silent time at meals
with such young ones
brings flexibility

Sitting in circle
at Be-In ending
Bonding warmth
transformation

Through rain and sun
we all become
extended family
Playfully Together

28 August 2012

PHAP VU'S TEACHINGS

Radical acceptance
of mind the way it is
Intimately knowing
from watching view

Wondrous teaching
of Radical Acceptance
Seeing more deeply
the full package deal

Pattern repeated
feeding the sore
Delusion that I'm
source of all suffering

If I was perfect
could make it all better
But then, of course
wouldn't be human

Yet in the Oneness
such beauty awaits
Birdsong calls out
I accept compassion

Break-through's illusion
Bubble burst insight
It's just an idea
Setting myself up

What a relief
Nothing but practice
Morning light through clouds
Sun streaming out

*   *   *

7 September 2012

ORDER OF INTERBEING RETREAT

Deepening Our Practice
each joining to enact
With such intension
we resonate accord

Wondrous Sangha
boundless, diverse
Right effort builds
flow of grace

Beach at sunrise
Meditation hall
Touching path
Singing together

We are one
as never before
OI breakthrough
with mindful being

Sister Annabel's teachings
through actions and words
supports our Indra's Net
Jewels reflecting one another

Doesn't matter if we suffer
but what we do about it
Patience of bigger heart
best self protection

Calming the mind
nothing can harm you
Sharing true harmony
lights way to Nirvana

*   *   *

Pure Land includes fear
Dear spasm clenching heart
Letting go of conflict
Nothing left for worry

Insect munching
on purple flower
Roadside splendour
offered to sacred

Bee collects pollen
Eye consciousness
Here in stillness
beauty unfolds

Dead golden flower
still smiles to sun
Seeds blow on
easing release

Heart softens
Bird calls through
Wind whooshes out
what still held

'If this isn't Pure Land
then what is?'
Sister Annabel smiles
I feel it too

*   *   *

Mommy, Daddy in me
we touch the earth
Laying upon you
difficulties so old

Traps of guilt
burning inside
carried for centuries
Now put down

Pouring on you
steady transformer
false responsibility
illusion of control

Guts so tight
slowly loosen
Such relief
with Bodhisattva

Then our Ceremony
remembering parents
Stones for shrine
Letter to you, burnt

Smoke rising
into new way
So much easier
releasing blame

We are much more
love coming through
Healing to nourish
for all generations

*   *   *

Magic on beach
led by True Virtue
Meditating together
as waves break on shore

Clear deathless nature
pebbles roll through
Birds fly in formation
Moon watches fully

We are one with all
sitting as a Sangha
Beyond time
life force through

Touching dried seabed
Vibration strong
Melting back to mother
I am not afraid

Life is vivid
as we return
Sheep so natural
We seem the same

8 September 2012

10 September 2012

FRUITS OF FOUR RETREATS

Taking in sustenance
of four retreats
Amazing teaching
learning and being

Sister Annabel
wisdom and hug
Deep, soft, focus
resonating through

Patience best protection
allowing bigger heart
Staying with now beauty
peace naturally embraces

Allowing change
at deeper level
True Virtue inspires
transformation at base

Joyfully Together
Family Retreat
Such special bond
with Sophie, Kerin

Annual event
us sharing love
Comfortable fun
Accepting each other

New Barn landscape
linking both retreats
Needing focused practice
sorting OI programme

Lighter release
of 'should be my way'
The more I let go
the easier life is

Polishing inner jewel
with Mindfulness, Reiki
Allowing it to shine
with effortless effort

In Net of Indra
each knot ties
jewel to radiate
on one another

Like mirrors on mirrors
natural reflections
Glow from each gem
made from them all

Together gleaming
each on the other
Sangha luminance
brightens so well

Mesh intertwined
in four dimensions
More than connection
one big white light

Steady practice
freshens this jewel
with living dharma
Vibration cleans, heals

11 September 2012	12 September 2012
DYSLEXIC FAMILY STREAM	*BABY SITTING ELLA TO SUPPORT KEV IN LONDON*

Understanding compassion
for our dyslexic stream
Family history
opening to change

Fear of not good enough
failure, kids laughing
confidence undermined
Wanting to do it right

Hard work antidote
seeming the way
extra time, care
just to make sure

Kev's Master's thesis
detailed, complex
Needing deep clarity
he already has

My experience
in similar position
Stable heart wide
Understanding, compassion

Red ripe raspberry
there in my heart
Kevin and Ella
both so alive

Wondrous contact
supportive connection
Helena holding
Bob and I backup

Bringing us all
such glowing feel
Intergenerational
vivid sharing

Being family
helping each other
Knowing we're there
shining on one another

Kevin's dissertation
nearly finished
His focused effort
coming to fruition

Bob and I
playing roles
Watching Ella
special time together

Her drawing, chatting
Walking with Bob
She's also focused
Understanding through art

Wishing them well
Enjoying contact
Sweetness of fruit, seeds
Red ripe raspberry

17 September 2012 (5773)   20 September 2012

NEW YEAR 5773

Happy New Year
Jewish, of course
Sun shining through
autumn breeze

Freshness of start
deepening release
of not good enough
Trying too hard

Doing so well
growing so much
Loved-ones too
I am so grateful

Walking this path
feet touching earth
Future goes own way
built on the present

Heart softening
beyond control
Smiling to thoughts
can't know what's best

What I can do
seeing beyond self
is open to life
step round cow dung

In this Pure Land
of Stourbridge Common
Rosh Hashanah blessings
New Year 5773

Kevin recovering
Finished dissertation
Masters Mazel Tov
arise from ancestors

As cattle are herded
away for the slaughter
I see lorry rocking
hear moos from inside

What I can do
is send Reiki love
for scared creatures
those who do roundup

Calm in shaky boat
Presence of steps
on Stourbridge Common
as sun streaks through

Autumn has come
New Year again
Kev back at college
Grandkids at school

As Bob and I pack
preparing for Salema
We share celebration
of completion with son

This summer's life
never same again
So precious together
savouring family

29 September – 10 October 2012

SALEMA, PORTUGAL POEMS

Salema quiet
sinking in
Recovery time
Returning again

Full moon on rocks
leading the way
Water so white
reflecting the trail

*   *   *

First ocean swim
so invigorating
Washing away
a year's gook

Wondrous as it's been
since last swim here
Still something special
being back in watery home

Swimming with sea gulls
floating on ripples
I slowly paddle by
Waves sing their splash

*   *   *

Village awakens
to sun breaking clouds
Tractor ready on shore
to pull up the boats

*   *   *

Dinosaur tracts re-exposed
falling on Salema beach
on its way to extinction
Back to sand once more

But for now a symbol
of fishing village time travel
Layered in slabs compressed
expanding as we witness

*   *   *

Bob so tan, relaxed
Skin contrasted
in turquoise tee shirt

Sea Gulls fly overhead
We swim together
laughing in the sea

26 October 2012

It's a miracle Kerin says
as we pass her old flat
That I was so ill
and now I'm much better

Yes, dear mind of mine
I want to shift the rut
from those angst feelings
to gratefulness of now

All how you look at things
Mom used to say
and I want to see
This is what I desired

Beyond my hopes then
that she could be so well
Though her special needs
will certainly continue

That takes special patience
and giving extra support
But she's lost a stone in weight
and is trying in own way

With wide perspective
I can find happiness
Releasing old view
Allowing in clear vision

For in that dark time
when this seem unimaginable
It was more than my dreams
This miracle of our ride

28 October 2012

With dissertation done
Kev's much more relaxed
Came away for a week
on half term with Ella

Such a special man
So very sincere
Hardworking, energetic
father and son

Ella growing tall
calmer, more focused
Speaking her own mind
Drawing out her world

Being Grandma Joy
Mom, Bob's partner
I open to warm waves
of blessing of this life

So much to be grateful
Family growing strong
Sophie, Kerin tomorrow
Savouring this still moment

A chance for perspective
of all we've accomplished
Ancestors look on
mitzvah of our love

31 October 2012

Sophie, Ella for two days
The girls bond so well
Culminating in circus
Kev takes Kerin, daughters

So much love, laughter
girls' secrets together
Kerin buys them gifts
Each of us grows

5 November 2012

Dusting off Mom
and Dad photos
compassion rupa
on windowsill

Returning to study
Peace to meditate
Space, tee tree oil
burning cleansing release

Touching Mom's hand
You're here in my own
After wondrous family visit
coming back to still clarity

There in Mom's eyes
I find your happiness
When, as young family
you came to visit us

Smiling to me now
across time and space
We settle back together
Dusting off Mom

10 November 2012

Beyond needing to be needy
allowing light to burn through
transforming the pain cluster
as it's consumed in fire

Being the conduit I am
letting Reiki energy through
to deeper levels of blocks
where my fear still cowers,

Kindness for that scared child
afraid she won't cope
with difficulties life brings
for loved-ones so dear

Trusting enough to believe
they too can grow in own ways
Their life lessons a catalyst
for potential spiritual maturity

My fear is but a block
both for them and myself
only in release can flame build
within myself, shining out

15 November 2012

Birthday fun with Kev
on the South Bank
Museum together
Chatting at café

View of the Thames
rippling beyond time
Chanukah past/future
Intergenerational

How to be Jews we are
beyond Israel, religion
Passing on culture
that feels right to us

Walking along the river
hearing of Kev's students
His projects with them
Their life changing chance

Hugging so happy
Masters Distinction
deserved from hard work
He thanks for our help

Taking his arm
man of thirty-five
Looking young, handsome
joking of slight balding

I remember babe in arms
feeding on rocking chair
listening to Beethoven
we played at his birth

Now this special day
Family dinner at Dim Sum
Ella brings doggy candles
for mango pudding cake

Celebrating together
three generations
father, teacher, artist
Birthday love with Kev

19 November 2012

*MINDFULNESS DAY
RESONATES*

Sangha warmth
Clearing brain
Practicing again
as never before

Special homey feel
sharing once more
our life difficulties
eased by being heard

Dear old friends
as we all age
energy of practice
softens our way

Sitting in harmony
being Sangha mind
Reciting the trainings
we all want to live

Eating, hugging
deeply walking
Touching earth
Releasing to mother

1 December 2012

If this isn't Pure Land
then what is?
True Virtue's question
brings light on life now

Warm hug with Bob saying
Can't think of nicer person
to be sleepless with in night
brings feel of our blessings

Poems in Here & Now
of summer retreats
with offspring then OI
in photos jointly smiling

24 November 2012

Smoke rising from houseboat
on first frosty morn
Long green expanse
topped with soft white

Mist from my breath
Chill in the air
Beauty of winter
neighbour and kids

Cycle ride out
into the Fens
Body warms
as I pedal

Along muddy river
quick flowing from rains
Flood protection
raises water level

Toward Fen Ditton
marshlands return
Lake grows anew
on saturated land

Sea gulls glide
above wide vista
In natural rhythm
I cycle on

Past three horses
still in wet field
fingertips chill
so I start back

Rowers wait turns
for chance to race
Supporters gather
Cheers are heard

Returning home
greeted by warmth
Hot cup of tea
Smoke rising slowly

27 November 2012

Moving Kerin's bed
Rearranging toward light
May Reiki flow
to us all today

May I have patience
wisdom and clarity
to release control need
Just be there to help

Embracing my fear
and need to be loved
Seeing Kerin has same
Compassion for us both

28 November 2012

Bodhisattva actions
build on each other
But I must reinforce
with daily practice

Us helping Kerin
move bed, clear
clutter in flat
Group energy flows

Seeing her life
in a new way
At home with Steph
them happily sorting

Feeding my heart
Her beyond stress
Clarifies my limits
when to step back

6-12 December 2012

WINTER GLIMPSES

Savouring sun's glow
upon eyes and body
Daylight energy
in short supply

Swans graze on grass
with cattle gone
Bare trees allow
brightness through

Soon solstice'll be here
slowly shifting darkness
Earth's cycles turning
back to the light

*　　　*　　　*

Thankful for our heating
after it packed up
Grateful repaired
Taking in warmth

Talking with Liz
Sharing with Sangha
Hugging Phung
Appreciating friends

*　　　*　　　*

Chanukah is cool
granddaughters say
My heart swells
with ancestor delight

Family gathers
for celebration
Once again together
Each being own self

Every candle different
bringing unique flame
When girls light them all
glow greater than parts

*　　　*　　　*

Two doves on bare tree
in white sky light
undisturbed by rain
Midwinter peace

Two of us inside
Writing, meditating
In warmth of fullness
resonating with life

13 December 2012

Intimate Bob birthday
with Kevin and I
Chatting in café
as coffee roasts

Sweet connection
flowing through
Warmth of being
intergenerational

Father and son
bond so close
In their faces
seeing resemblance

Working on projects
Fannie's site, books
Social scientists
Faithful family men

Blanketed in love
wrapping us all
in interwoven
heartfelt life

Off to museum
Pre-Raphaelites
Enjoying, discussing
Sharing favourites

Walking by river
with my best guys
Sun breaks through
in unity of strength

18 December 2012

Beyond Evil Eye
will see, revenge
Happy, grateful
not caught in binds

Telling family
ancestors deep
Kevin's photo
won an award

Allowing happiness
to resonate out
Smiling to jinx
Old fear to transform

The future's a river
flowing unknown
But happiness now
feeds rippling currents

19-29 December 2012

Advising client
to feed the positive
I tell myself
with new perspective

Seeing in her
the negative spin
brings such suffering
stagnation, confusion

Feeling that energy
then Reiki clearing
Rippling through body
bringing deep relief

As she sighs
releases, letting go
throat charka opens
allowing healing through

Looking so much better
after the treatment
She glimpses perspective
to create affirmation

*   *   *

Giving Reiki
as darkness falls
on shortest day
Mayan changeover

Good sign client says
We both agree
Higher consciousness
for a new era

Time to rest
visit, enjoy
family and friends
let the holidays begin!

*   *   *

Jessie writes from prison
Hope holiday greetings
find you healthy, happy
bounded by friends, loved-ones

Struck by how I am
The contrast salient
though he's cheerful
Each accepting own lives

Our winter party last night
Annual turning toward light
Sharing food with friends
reconnecting with warmth

Catching up on our lives
serving out and washing
Bob tells of coffee research
Such interest is sparked

Richness of family
visiting these Hols
Sophie, Kerin today
Kev, Ella next week

A chance to enrich
our intertwined beings
Compassionate Detachment
allows energy flow through

1 January 2013

Courage to be Bodhisattva
worry whirlpools and all
Allowing the sun through
to heal into depths of fear

Confidence to touch mother ground
with my whole body,
steps resonate Buddha nature
energy easily streams easy

Faith that flow is safe
witnessing its work before
Letting go into Indra's net
where I fall back into Oneness

Daring to notice Find The Worst
Seeing spiral with detachment
through compassionate eyes
where it transforms to earth symbol

Belief that I can do it
represent dear Thay
in whatever ways life brings
Starting with my inner landscape

Assurance mind change is possible
Seeing the shifts already done
Ungrasping judgement spin
to allow authentic Joy

Flying above the clouds
with wings spread wide open
Gliding on the currents
above the sea and beyond

There in effortless effort
unity brings release
Relaxing into own skin
Courage to be Bodhisattva

5 January 2013

Feeding satisfied, happy
Thay peace, open heart
so pleased in sleepless night
that 'Life is good' arises

Resonating with beauty
my only job, nice work
Allowing sweet energy
to embrace the pain

Retraining my brain
Clearness of true goal
Allowing contentment
to fill my being

Feeling fullness
of still, foggy morn
Tea tree steam floats
into my head

Sitting next to Thay
there all the time
His mind to my heart
joyful effusion

Practicing with Sangha
concentration builds
Needing deep focus
facilitating last night

This is it now
just as it is
Breathing into achy
relaxed body

6 January 2013

Sophie is here
in family embrace
Stability surrounds
creative endeavour

She reads aloud
Kerin, Kev's stories
Helping Ella write
Sophie does the same

The muse is flowing
following mind stream
to her own creations
The thrill, excitement

Automatic writing
naturally blooms
There in Sophie
in time of need

Therapeutic
renovation
Imagination flows
through fingers to page

So grateful to be
a part of process
enabling granddaughter
to express herself

Family occupation
creative energy
runs through Sophie
in her unique way

So negative spin
rewound other way
Remoulding confusion
into love's transformations

6 January 2013

WRITTEN FOR FANNIE'S 100TH BIRTHDAY

Celebrating Fannie
feeling part of nature
Resonating with beauty
depicted in your art

Creative life
Transformation
Interwoven with Ed
still inside you

Together within us
Your kindness, care
showered on grandchildren
Such generous sharing

Allowing us growing time
Encouraging inner muse
Inspirational example
Holding high justice torch

That light has been passed
to your children and theirs
You shine in all you touched
your energies glow on

*   *   *

Making Snow Fannie
Website together
Celebrating special lady
turning one-hundred

SKYPEing beyond
distance separation
Seeing her again
with SF family

Stream of love
through generations
Warmth healing
misunderstandings

In bigger picture
good intensions
feed caring feelings
of our closeness

All pitching in
baking as she did
Great-grandchildren
now lick the spoons

Her creative muse
blooms in new forms
of writing, photos
visual arts

Fannie, Ed's justice
drive, activism
Expressed through us
in innovative ways

All living part
of greater whole
Whiteness within
Making Snow Fannie

14 January 2013

After reciting
14 Mindful Trainings
Reiki Share
TOIC teleconference

Snowing Lotus Seeds
Cool white surrounds
yellow Jasmine flowers

Tree lightly covered
Two Doves still sit
beyond any fear

Kernels gently falling
through passage to depth
where doubt still remains

I can see you
for what you are
mere habit emotion

Energy spin
in wrong direction
Old guilt malaise

But blackness of mud
shows your true value
for transformation

Allowing such kindness
of blossom potential
brings understanding

There they fall
upon rich soil
for rejuvenation

18 January 2013

After touching earth
in morning exercises
Twenty-one spins round
Standing with Buddha

Love embracing
pain accepted
In hollow of heart
understanding grows

Holding, holding
with generosity
my intimate fears
loved-ones' problems

Wishing it were different
that they were pain free
All I can really do
is transform my own

In this process
space is cleared
to accept them as is
Love embracing

24 January 2013

After seeing/hearing
London Klezmer Quartet
and Jewish Socialists
in Sholem Aleykhem Comrade!

Nourishing Yiddish
Klezmer resonates
deep into root
thirsty for home

Guttural Singsong
vibrates to core
Feeling so comfy
it's a *Machia*

Violin, clarinet
Accordion, voice
We happily join in
part of greater whole

Still in the music
sob, caught in throat
In spite of suffering
trills and dancing

Touching so deeply
that vivid emotion
Arms wide open
Loud belly laugh

Glowing Oneness
mother tongue unspoken
Melody lingers on
in new generations

Diaspora home
here within
Worldwide connection
Nourishing Yiddish

Sholem Alaykhem
Peace to you all
Diaspora message
spread across globe

Interconnection
beyond isolation
Integrating, yet
keeping Jewish spirit

Being *Mensch*
Mitzvahs flow
through peaceful living
Sholem Aleykhem

*   *   *

7 – 13 February 2013

Returning from visit
sweet London time
Women's Lib sisters
Deep old connections

Mom within
genes, advice
in body cells

Wearing Mom's swimsuit
just after she passes
Friends recognise her

Help me please
strength and courage
to be True Self

In mind freedom
plasticity remolds
Showing inner smile

There all the time
since before birth
appearance cloaked

Now seeing clearer
beyond vision limits
Beauty's so vivid

*   *   *

Childhood feeling
too scary to look at
that death/life cycle
severs from parents

But now still connected
in deeper understanding
Gentle safety of being
sun, cloud, air, earth

*   *   *

Tendon inflammation
Reiki to Hara, spreading
Softening between exercise
Breathing in patient healing

Phung's kind treatment
being there when needed
Such a Bodhisattva
as a kind human being

17 February 2013

Picking up family
kids and grand
Each cooperating
in their own way

Girls so close
sharing secrets
Kev and Kerin
join in together

Kev, Ella staying on
for week's holiday
Energy so welcome
Happiness spreads

Such good intensions
keeps us going well
Family sharing
Oneness of our genes

*   *   *

Resting in now
birdsong and bangs
Feet on the stairs
generations through

Kevin so fresh
not burdened by past
Together we feel
his childhood eyes

Kind and gentle
just like the name
Suddenly his daughter
is the one who's seven

Life cycle repeats
right before me
Wondrous resonation
our sharing provides

Ella and I sew
Relaxing us both
Mom surely there
teaching us well

Hide the knot
wisdom passed on
Serenity waves
carrying through

19 February 2013

Family time together with Kevin and Ella colouring our lives in vivid beauty

It's the way you paint things
Kev says in kitchen sun
Understanding deeply
at level of mind

Reminiscent vibration
of Mom's same insight
All the way you look at things
Generations come back round

Breathing in wisdom
allowing awareness shift
For happiness in life
by finding the best

Yesterday with Ella
slowly walking by river
singing Happiness
Is Here And Now

Dropping worries
she likes that song
Can understand alive now
not in past or future

From this mindset
I'm not bothered
spending an hour
on fifteen minute walk

She climbs on low walls
We admire gliding birds
Someone must be feeding
as they all swarm by

Yes, she finds them
and asks so nicely
if she could also
throw them some bread

After Ella feeds them
ducks follow us
as we walk on
in warmth of sun

Finding stone
to draw on pavement
Tapping on railings
sounds play a song

No where to go
Nothing to do
No longer in
a hu-r-r-y

Buying used stamps
at Oxfam shop
Like I got Sophie
Ella wants the same

Who do we meet
but Sophie's auntie
Ella sings to aunt
Older ladies clap

Munching in cake shop
afternoon complete
Back on the bus
Kev writing funding app

He and Helena
working for justice
Ed, Fannie so pleased
their energies continue

So many blessings
Kerin's doing better
in her own way
when I drop expectations

25 February 2013

After Wondrous Chaos
of family surround
Savouring stillness
birdsong serenade

Eight days of grandkids
grown children et all
So glad we could host
Well enough to enjoy

Pushing kids on rides
in winter chill of park
Walking by river
Drawing, imagining

Puppets and singing
helps Ella understand
worries just in mind
We're only alive now

Barbie tells teddy
better happy than not
Rino demonstrates
digging fear hole

Play therapy
helps me as well
to choose the beauty
above tangled regret

Dearest Bob
giving to all
now settles back to write
We make a good team

Recognising Bodhisattva
This being called Joy
No one else can do it
Only I can truly see

Recognising Bodhisattva
for what I am
Not the same person
that I was before

Recognising Bodhisattva
Evolving as I grow
in Reiki resonation
for me, family, all

Recognising Bodhisattva
Feeding her well
with this deep knowing
Expansive from core

Recognising Bodhisattva
Watching so clearly
how this is true reality
Beyond external factors

Recognising Bodhisattva
for what she is
this beautiful being
manifest in body/mind

Recognising Bodhisattva
not ashamed to be good
in genuine life stream
Enjoying the way

Seeing Bodhisattva in fear
Sudden glimpse clarity
Light into such depths
bringing gentle compassion

Instant by instant alive
Millisecond of breath
Distinct yet in the flow
Washing clear through chest

What is there to be scared of
when I can attend this closely
Heart engulfing spacious
remnants of old habits

Greenness of equanimity
shining through to brain
where plasticity realigns
Seeing Bodhisattva in fear

*   *   *

4 – 5 March 2013

6 March 2013

Knocked over by wave
swirled in its energy
of helpless despair
I rise again

Feeling as well
Sweet family surround
Bob's loving care
He also has limits

Seeing my limits
patience worn thin
Loved-one's dependency
once more sucks me in

Loving me enough
to stay this intimate
Even in despair
I mother you gently

*   *   *

Heart breaks open
catching negative spin
with useful result
exposing more mud

Such muck and mire
brought to the surface
to be transformed
Reminding of essential

Thanks to good friends
who listen and share
Reiki, difficulties
Energy cleansing each

So many years
we've met this way
Together once more
is such a blessing

Reciting 14 Mindful Trainings
SKYPing together in beauty
With OI Sisters and Brothers
interconnecting through space

Bringing Thay's teachings home
This snow covered spring
In UK and Cyprus
sharing our commitment

Being more myself
allowing less self-conscious
concern about offending
Either too big or small

Beyond blocking worry
of Sangha judgement
As nothing to become
can truly be me

Cell of Sangha body
letting true voice through
Brooklyn accent and all
American Jewish sister

7 March 2013

After clearing sit
at Phouc and Phung's
We all profit
from focusing together

Purple violets blossom
from depth of heart break
Opening and opening
in freshness anew

Staying with instant
that each one buds
in the next moment
another flourishes

Allowing the beauty
trust and belief
to grow on through
anxiety veil

The best I can do
for Loved-one and I
is be flower blooming
in spirit and being

8 March 2013

INTERNATIONAL WOMEN'S
DAY

Mother Nature
Earth provider
allowing life force
generations old

Back to great plans
of ancient Asia
Turkic ancestors
travel together

Trusting the Goddess
families slowly cross
Suckling new baby
cradling on back

Feminine Nurture
we celebrate today
Courage returns
Mom's Common Sense

20 March 2013

Swallow springs slowly
Puppet Centre demise advice
Discouraging turning point
which reshaped my life

This time older, wiser
Healing source of hurt heart
way back to non-beginnings
where survival/change interplay

Kindness to confusion
Asking why's just second arrow
Better watch and reconcile
into fresh blooming

Bodhisattva Courage
Not knowing path ahead
But direction is clear
That's where I shall go

Towards life's beauty
beyond planning worry
Seeing, embracing
Continuing with Reiki

Not sure what'ill happen
though not as expected
Smiling to expectations
Looking to reality

Mom's advice so good
feeling her with me
So long ill in hospital
I breathe easy for us both

This is my opportunity
surprise adventure now
Not needing to know
Only follow the light

Wisdom shines new day
I open heart to embrace
my own special path
Enjoying possibilities

Later I'll look back, see
where this turning point led
For now I just need trust
the wondrous dharma body

Don't want to miss chance
to resonate with Ultimate
beyond recognition
in quiet, steady steps

Acknowledging my practice
brings courage to continue
in Great Bright Light direction
Swallowing springs slowly

*   *   *

Reiki Master teaching
takes on new meaning
Sensi's enlightenment
shines out to us

Great Bright Light
for me and students
practicing together
Resonating being

In concentration
passing attunements
Reiki mindset
Oneness to whole

Transformation
Light penetration
Healing heart
helps us all

Ella says don't know what to do
on this first day of her holiday
I teach her improvisation
which she already lives well

Yes, she'll do that in park
with trees and play equipment
Not always needing a script
I tell her, reminding myself

Releasing plan I had in mind
to discover more intuition
Opening heart to happiness
while embracing fear there

Dear Amygdala reaction
coming to see you more clearly
In Prefrontal wider view
allowing wisdom to descend

*   *   *

Ella in green dress
long hair like mine
Focused, creative artist
Laughing after cartwheels

Kevin works with Ella
to spell out first e-address
The one that she wants is
Happiness is Here and Now
Thanks for the reminder

Family Passover
Girls help prepare
seder plate items
chopping and mixing

Now old enough
to understand
read and partake
in ancient ceremony

Jews were slaves
Let no one be now
True Liberation
best for us all

Everyone has feelings
Don't want to forget
Inside each person
goodness still shines

On Exodus *Matzah*
We put our *Haroses*
Remembering slavery
and sweetness of freedom

As we rekindle
kinship tradition
Such warmth for all
Celebrating together

Play made by cousins
harkens back to mine
Relatives gathering
in new generations

All those from past
happily partake
Power flowing through
stream of traditions

13 April 2013

Bob asks last night
how often in cosmos
two people together
as contented as us

Such special blessing
I do want to savour
Us safe in living room
hearing/speaking truths

Him in soft chair
as never before
yet so recognisable
for forty-five years

Hurt and loving
earnest, concerned
for my well being
as I am for him

Shifting moment
of built up resentments
Also life changes
and new beginnings

Wanting to be
so beyond striving
Exploration deep
but also free, wide

He ask sincerely
do I really know
what I am doing
and why doing it

Questions to step back
from assumption edge
Catching my balance
to gain perspective

Care about Sangha
Thay says important
Do find joint energy
has special power

But pulled along
from loyalty to Thay
with assumed idea
of what I should do

Many ways to live
teach and learn
the Dharma path
to true awakening

Sister who stayed home
dug farm with focus
found the true treasure
her father had left them

Remembering clarity
of true mind present
No need to go seek
what's already here

My path's unclear
and covered with hurt
misperceptions of
what others will think

May you slowly clear
this tribal sort of haze
I'd been drawn into
and only now realise

Giving me time/space
to heal into myself
Return to true source
Release wilfulness

16 April 2013	17 April 2013
Reiki flow heals	Puppet Baby Reiki
red, green, purple	Perfect combination
Allowing energy	Merging of skills
to go its own way	past/present interests
Waiting for washer	And best of all
new client calls	helpful to toddler
Shifting direction	Digestive system
to treating mum, baby	taking in much healing
Movement happening	Little-one sat
Bob and I book	for so very long
flight to Barcelona	as powerful Reiki
Then flat won't work	softened, eased tummy
Clearly this morning	Mum felt the difference
best to book another	Bloating subsided
A bit more expensive	Happy little child
but better for us	raises arms with smile
After so stuck	She so connected
confused and hurt	to puppets that heal
Fresh opportunities	Waving to them
in unimagined ways	as my finger waves back
	What satisfying fun
	and helpful to Mum
	Now wants to learn Reiki
	to help baby, herself

20 April 2013

Baking with Sophie
as she turns ten
Making her cake
sharing kitchen warmth

Her staying over
relaxed in our house
So a part of family
just as I'd hoped

Such a good kid
Self-possessed as ever
Licking the bowl
with joyful smile

Liking pastry making
reading and writing
Finding her way
with extended family

Telling three parties
one here with Kerin
Sunday with friends
Dad's side on Tuesday

Happy opportunities
grow with granddaughter
Our special relationship
Baking with Sophie

21 April 2013

Starry gratitude
once quiet returns
after Sophie, Cat party
birthday together

Accepting blessings
both are doing well
in their own way
with family surround

Sophie and Ella
climb trees, tell secrets
Kev and Kerin
go for walk, talk

Bob and I
well to create
space and care
for celebration

But energy dip
leaves us tired
Preparing for trip
Hope to rest on beach

27 April 2013

Life in colour
in busy Barcelona
Stripes and plaids
gracefully intermingle

Broken tiles
into mosaics
Gaudi creates
fantasyland

Breaking the rules
of what goes together
Allowing imagination
to freely wander

Miro transforms
war and repression
with graceful squiggles
in brightness of life

Barcelona spirit
Catalonian flags
Books and Roses
for Sant Jordi day

Bob and I in
adventure mode
Ups and downs
flowing together

A chance to explore
inner/outer worlds
from fresh perspective
Energy sharing

Such a pleasure
Return to quiet life
past travelling hassles
Absorbing inspiration

1-2 May 2013

THE TAI CHI WAY

Freeing Release
Not my arm or body
Moving past will
feeling deeper source

Beyond gripping struggle
Mike easily frees arm
In one fluid twist
Not at all bothered

The Tai Chi way
just as Buddha
Past grasping/aversion
is just letting go

Investing in loss
of ego as well
Expectations, illusions
slowly dismantle

Spring pressed way down
begins to rebound
As leaves bud on branches
still supple in wind

Yes, rooted down
but beyond rigid
Kind understanding
allows inner compassion

Sun breakthrough
to clear blue sky
Tai Chi warms chill
Birds serenade

From nurturing earth
movement arises
Flowing through air
as if it were water

From base of solidity
body can soften
More easily recognise
tightness, fear, worry

There on left side
old habits grasp
Judgement can squeeze heart
Good, that I noticed

I want you to be well
dear valuable body pump
Keeping blood circulating
with Ki/Chi as well

*   *   *

3 May 2013

So proud of you, Helena
Your Phd efforts
to understand, record
lives of Irish Women

Such harsh difficulties
repression and famine
Yet such strong spirit
to nurture the children

As old Women's Libber
of 1970's, 80's
I participated in struggles
against our oppression

Eventually I saw
that caught in old binds
held by aversion
to what I repulsed

While rejecting the rules
of Male Chauvinist game
identity still entrapped
in established mindset

How to step back
truly break shackles
Gain clearer vision
Freedom of being

Creative endeavours
like Feminist books
Art space to explore
New ways of living

Slowly it dawned on me
that being gripped by anger
held me in their game plan
I needed to let go

Having to prove right
still played by their rules
Not explaining 'us' to 'them'
But just walking away

Feeling mother earth's
support beneath my feet
Being beauty of nature
is women's true birthright

Our power of re-creation
baby girls and boys
opens our hearts to all
We are their mothers

But most important
to be our own mothers
Nurture inner/outer wounds
to transform to freedom

Healing ourselves
to see through delusions
narrowing definitions
of who or what we are

From vast perspective
comes power of insight
Supporting our sisters
to control their mind/bodies

Through the great oceans
eroding ancient rock
new shapes emerge
beyond our plans

So what's it all about
as we women stride on
Each new generation
discovers for itself

I trust that within you
conclusions will bloom
to finish your dissertation
and relax in spring sun

My dear Helena
with a big hug
I embrace you with love
and power of completion

7 May 2013   8 May 2013

ORDER OF INTERBEING GATHERING

With fourfold Sangha   In warmth of our circle
in our sharing circle   at ease seeing panel
Heart opened so wide   of dharmacharya aspirants
soft, fresh and clear   from back of audience

Weekend retreat together   That's not my path
Dharma talks rain wisdom   but happiness is
Sister Bi leads us through   Following trainings
anger mindset transformation leaves unfold

Encouraging us to share   Supported in practice
how we live each training   by Anh's energy, words
Unpicking fourteen   Valuing my heart
Ceremoniously reunited   depth of sacrifice

Dear Michael, Phap Son   Her understanding
Speaks of communication   touching so deeply
intertwined with trust   Encouraging me purple
Needing to share deeper   'Spirituality suits you'

Our own Sister Natasha   Michael's advice
beaming from Thay travels   Thay says many things
Jetlagged from Thailand   If a thousand practitioners
Still joyfully skilled practice then that many teachers

Delicate awareness   Melting distrust
of sweet Anh Nghiem   with Sister Bi's guidance
Resonating solidity   Releasing obsessive thinking
way beyond words   to let go into healing

Expanding of Tulips   I know that I'm loved
encompassing OI, aspirants   as part of OI family
Knowing family better   Don't need to be formal teacher
Sister, brother and within   just be with awakening light

Forming flower hug
We sing as one being
Precept body grows
Blooming so wide

9 May 2013

Wind blowing through
ruminants still held
of dear affliction
fear, guilt, find worst

Softening to release
for me and ancestors
these blocking restraints
that it's all my fault

False responsibility
for other's suffering
holding me back
from love of True Self

Reality clearer
how I help others
but to do more
must start with myself

So I look deeper
seeing closer to root
Childhood scapegoating
of me by family

And beyond that
women's caring role
Taking on the pain
to make it all better

Seeing stuck bits
clinging to ribs
begin to float away
Wind blowing through

13 May 2013

Heaven now
Broad expanse
Heart widens
to take in affliction

'But I wanted
it to be my way
Yes, this is good
but not as I planned'

My dear old friend
I embrace you again
with understanding
in warm arms of love

Knowing fear's distraction
and this is your root
I feed you with beauty
of walking on Green

Sun breaking through
Cows rest on grass
gently chewing crud
I softly step past

Not needing to be perfect
More than enough bounty
to nourish my being
Heaven right now

Reiki Engaged Buddhism
Treatments and training
The way of awareness
through spiritual energy

Back to the founder
Tendai Buddhist priest
Passing on experience
of his enlightenment

'Better to share widely'
he taught the public
Spreading beyond Japan
through his open heart

Grateful for connection
to my childhood dream
If I could just touch them
and make it all better

Merely being conduit
for positive conditions
Life force power
helps body heal itself

Reiki shining into
blocks of stress, pain
Confusion clearing
allowing sun through

Penetrating clouds
of fear and delusion
Twists of old hate
generations old

Arriving with heavy load
Leaving so much lighter
Obstructions breaking up
Mirrored in client's smile

Of course, it takes life change
for patients' healing process
So introducing mindfulness
and learning self Reiki

From Mozambique to Iceland
Spain, Sweden, Poland
From Cambridge and villages
I'm happy to meet them

Students seek relief
Spiritual expansion
In transmission miracle
they renew to Reiki

This reconnection
to their true selves
allows such potential
Opening to Oneness

Feeling vibration
palms hot or cold
By end of first training
emitting for self, others

In Usui Sensei's wisdom
he taught how to practice
mindfulness, meditation
Which I can pass on

Opportunity to grow
deeply into present
This physical resonation
helps bring home to Now

18 May 2013

28 May 2013

The beauty of patience
wide space to breathe
Time to bless life
beyond hurry/worry

I want to cultivate
this garden of patience
for me and Loved-one
to enjoy day together

Seeing tangled resentment
grow as I'm kept waiting
Transformed into Reiki
to work with the energy

I am worthy of love
back to childhood feel
Young girl walking through storm
in Newark with social troubles

Taking comfort from song
Holding head high though confused
knowing that time would pass
Bright silver sky yet to come

Transforming embedded thorns
Popularity problems, put-downs
Laughed at for being 'so good'
Worried might have bad breath

Bija still in Store Consciousness
activated by conditions now
Giving space to be aired
lotus seeds shower old pain

Most important work I can do
being here for ten year old Joy
Sending Reiki back to difficulties
patiently letting scar tissue heal

4 June 2013

I awoke and wrote this
in unusual pattern
Coming up from restless sleep
the truth jells, manifests

I take back my power
Connection to Unconditioned
This is my time
Mom says to use wisely

She had her life
growth and sharing
I continue with mine
Shining out for family

Rahelly says Kev's ability
to re-frame difficulties
he got from me
I hadn't recognised

Been caught in old pattern
of relinquishing my power
to 'authorities' for recognition
When what I want's right here

Trying to please them
as I'm used as scapegoat
Finding ways to reconcile
from capacity of awareness

No need to fight them
nor, of course, give in
Each side is attachment
I breath and walk free

Rediscovering authenticity
from depth of my being
This collage called Joy
I value your energies

Rebuilding confidence
in my own abilities
Trusting wondrous essence
Using positive kindness

5 June 2013

Remembering my own hell
and how I grow and learn
I wrote this for a friend

Content changes
but process the same
Transforming negative
energy to positive

So much growth
in the practice
Clarity, power
arising out of need

Pain's incentive
going through hell
Needing stability
A way to truly cope

Roots so deep
touching the earth
so branches can sway
without breaking in storm

Great motivation
to release to peace
Healing heart
to let it reopen

Coming out other side
with so much depth
Not wanting this trial
but profiting all the same

8 June 2013

SOPHIE SLEEPOVER

Sophie reads, I meditate
House peaceful and still
Warmth coming through
spreading for us both

She wants to be a writer
Just for the fun of it
Beyond making money
Sophie likes to do it

So happy for her
growing abilities
She has the knack
for creative word sharing

Always self possessed
That inner stability
carrying her through
into life's beauty

I wish you such wellness
Getting tall, expanding
May you be safe, happy
mindfully successful

10 - 11 June 2013

Heart opening to this hybrid
blossoming in wild purple buds
Knowing some would call 'weed'
but beauty shines beyond words

Jewish flower of Diaspora
able to live in many soils
Seeing past boundary lines
even if nation-states can't

Belonging, growing within
accepting me more and more
Moving beyond disturbances
of those who see me as 'outsider'

Thriving with friends who understand
coming from their own diversities
Though I know some can't conceive
of being British beyond fixed view

Nourishing this heart to open
to accept them, even if they don't me
Feeling roots down to Unconditioned
where we're all together as one

*　　　*　　　*

True Self shine through
beyond fear of non-acceptance
American and British
Jewish and Buddhist
Working and Middle Class

Woman, Mother, Gran
Dyslexic Poet
Unique Mind Connection
Reiki flooding through
for learning and growing

ARRHYTHMIA

ECG Normal though arrhythmia continues

Reiking miniature child
basking in healing sunlight
Feeling energy through

Awakened in such good place
realising little-one is me
Accepting my therapy powers

Easing into depth of release
Letting go as I did on table
being Reikied by Liz, Rahelly

Coming into soft space of being
Sitting down to meditate
Feeling heart pounding in chest

Releasing in heart centre
where palpitations persist
for restoring life through block

*   *   *

Heart pumping irregular
into chest centre
through Tai chi and Reiki
Decide to call Doctor

Appointment soon
to check mechanics
I think transformation
widening middle Hara

But better to know
Mike convinces
As it continues
I'd advise the same

*   *   *

Happy with me like this
scared kid and arrhythmia
Thankful ECG normal
Opening my heart

Seeing old pattern
suppressing my power
afraid will use wrongly
not good enough to trust

Hard to defend myself
Much easier defending others
Frightened inner child
Power too much or not enough

Letting go to process
way beyond my control
Embracing fearful little Joy
Happy with me like this

*   *   *

Practicing acceptance
as arrhythmia returns
while my fingers type
Beyond worry, just being

Rung Phung this morning
she'll see me on Thursday
All's well with love
Good practice this is

Reporting back to Bob
He hugs me so kindly
I savour this strawberry
of precious time together

20 – 25 June

Don't undermine Bodhisattva
Thay kindly encourages
to be happy with what is

Yesterday arrhythmia getting better
after focusing through Reiki Oneness
Connection to everything, which I am

Remembering sitting with Dad
After wheeling him out beyond hospital
'You've no idea how wonderful's fresh air'

Such a pleasure us breathing together
Overcoming Mom's difficulties too
in this deep filling of my lungs

Relishing this oxygen of life
Heart reminding, Time's Limited
All the more precious to enjoy

Phung tells me arrhythmia's from stress
Though I don't feel it; it's drip, drip
Eventually the glass spills over

I'm touched, knowing she's right
Great, wise healer that she is
I'm only one who can change my life

*   *   *

Equanimity asset
beyond results
Liking, loving me enough
to relax in nature's hands

Just as Mom found
her own peaceful state
Being in God's hands
her dying well rippled
I know that Mom wishes
me to find the same
In accepting myself
My own Serenity

*   *   *

Heart tests normal
arrhythmia subsiding
Doctor says occasional
asymptomatic

Don't do anything
not even aspirin
That's fine with me
Stop listening just relax

Learning from Phung
consider how less
stress in life possible
untangle, enjoy

Allowing heart to open
without heart disturbed
by difficulties of world
best way to help all

30 June 2013

26 July 2013

Written on OI retreat
training with Sister Annabel
on Faith in Practice

Surprised loved the silence
of 3 days nurturing space
Blossoming into insight

I am everywhere
Particles dispersed
as wave part of water
So illusion just here

Glimpse of realisation
After touching earth
Sister Annabel's talks
blowing me away

Energy all
though can take form
Comfort in silence
No need to materialise

Flower just blooms
with nothing to prove
In retreat safety
may I do the same

Trusting the practice
even if we're imperfect
More confidence in this person
with so many inner Buddhas

Just allowing space
for message to sink in
There's no self to suffer with
I am everywhere

Mom's tree died
Apple Canker it seems
Planted after she passed
Neighbour says now shows
she doesn't needed it anymore

Where have you gone
Yes, I do know
Back to ocean essence
Alive in your descendents
So present in me
A part of spiritual growth

Mom who transmitted
deep energy to this being
Serenity you found
manifests in my own way
You've no need for 'self'
spread throughout existence

In bigness of being
beyond any fear
You are so very free
that I have to smile
Enjoying breath together

So I let you go
as I do Joy ego
Loosening the bonds
into wider perspective
Where sorrows can melt
into new plant blossoms

29 July 2013

Arrhythmia solution
It turns out caused
by too much spinning
in Tibetan exercise

Twenty-one times limit
Phung says there's a reason
More is fun but overdoes it
Heart calmer with less

*   *   *

Teaching Reiki Mindfulness
to students I know well
Nurse finds wounds heal faster
Others fall asleep more quickly

Off to Allotment Barbeque
Rahelly says it's my idea
So lovely to meet diverse
other farmers - energised

2 August 2013

Day off with Bob
walking South Bank
Happy together
just sitting by river

Like old times
No agenda
Nothing to do
but just enjoy

Him working so hard
obsessed with new book
May it blossom wide
Selling to many

Me doing Reiki
preparing for retreat
with Kerin, Sophie
A unique challenge

Comforted by experience
of past Family Gatherings
Useful to them both
supported by the Sangha

Wanting to be
in right space to go
with patience and clarity
so energy flows well

May Reiki be with me
to keep my heart opened
Savouring Sophie's childhood
Kerin as special person

Giving myself now
loving encouragement
to just relax deeply
Recharging this being

3 August 2013

Shocked seeing Swastika
at war memorabilia stall
Flag is partly folded
Could it really be that?

Yes, says saleswoman
It's not illegal
I see Jews humiliated
as this flies overhead

But it's a Nazi symbol
No, we're not like that
We're Christians, she protests
I note her lack of history

Trying to explain
asking her nicely
to please remove this
She puts hand up, no!

I find my market friend
hearing inner cry
of woman's war agony
Friend says stall is like that

Her display glistens jewels
Crystals vibrate life force
She shrugs, what can we do?
And waits on next customer

Walking, touching earth
Feet feel solidity
I can't just go to café
so head to Guild Hall

At council office
I tell what I've seen
Although man listens
he doesn't seem surprised

Licences for stalls
don't specify what can sell
But, surely, here in Cambridge
we discourage Neo-Nazis

We're struggling against
English Defence League
coming from other cities
to stop mosque being built

Persisting, it comes out
the impetus which brought me
Coming from Jewish background
and what this represents

He goes to his computer
I guess to type my complaint
But then he finds a number
and dials upstairs

Um, there's a lady here
who wants to complain
about the market stall
that has a Swastika

The head of the market
will come down to see you
Just have a seat over there
I sit with visions of German Jews

We were powerless to complain
when the Nazis forced us
to scrub pavements as they jeered
Then gassed us in Auschwitz

Standing as Head appears
I explain I'm local resident
As stalls are licensed by council
it's responsible for what's displayed

We're working to make Cambridge
a multicultural, accepting city
I'm pleased council commemorates
Holocaust Remembrance Day

German Jews encourage me
We don't want horror repeats
Feeling their energy
I speak of being Jewish

Well, if it causes offence
I assure him it does
and did ask them nicely
to take symbol away

In moment of silence
war suffering surrounds
I breathe transformation
and wait with compassion

Stall Holder'll listen to me
Head is sure of that
Together we walk out
into sun of summer change

I stand by the buskers
as he approaches war objects
Watch contentious body language
Then Head finally returns

He'll put away swastika
but German memorabilia's
one of his best sellers
So he can make a sign
and show and sell if asked

After heartfelt thanks
feeling ripples of relief
flowing through generations
not having to relive horror

Back to my stall friend
She's pleased, surprised
at my direct action
I felt no choice being Jewish

I slowly cross the market
Don't want to be intimidated
to walk near memorabilia
where swastika's, thankfully, gone

Man follows, Excuse me
there's anger in his voice
I stop and he comes round
Stall owner confronts me

I listen with solidity
This is what he needs
A chance to be heard
Respected as a person

Don't want things hidden
but history remembered
Know so many Jews killed
Gypsies, too, and others

He calms as I agree
he's not personally a Nazi
Says customers just interested
in historical value

I tell him of Jewish heritage
how symbol is offensive
Neo-Nazis on the rise
through parts of Europe

My customers aren't like that
They buy expensive authentic
Good jobs, well healed people
That other kind get replicas

Anyone can be a Fascist
but you're in a good position
to tell them of symbol meaning
and what Nazi's did

Yeah, I know all about that
I watched The World at War
All twenty six episodes
I'm not a holocaust denier

Of course, that's important
We want multicultural Cambridge
He asks if I live here
Yes, foreign accent, but British

He's had a swastika on stall
most days of last five years
His Granddads fought in war
for freedom to sell memorabilia

But just as we don't allow
racist slurs to be said to people
Swastikas carry same meaning
building hatred, division

The Germans were just people
I think of Dresden and agree
So many families killed
As pacifist, I want no harm

I assure him I hadn't object
to his business as a whole
but Nazi symbol's offensive
He says not trying to do that

Yes, I realise not your intension
I can see you didn't mean that
But the kind of offence caused
does make it truly offensive

By now he's not threatened
There's areas we won't agree on
He can see my point of view
but can I see his?

I understand, though don't agree
and I do wish him well
Then he sticks out his hand
and I calmly shake it

19 August 2013

FAMILY RETREAT

Sowing Seeds Together
in myself and family
on our annual retreat
New Barn once again

Granddaughter takes Two Promises
wrapped in great-grandma's shawl
Says she wants to be aware
of how lucky we are

Her Mum blooms wide
in accepting support
Friends water her flower
Good to talk with Cat

Valuing three generations
with words, smiles and eyes
Connecting in our love
Expressed out in the open

Each Sangha flower watered
in the nurturing circle
So happy for one another
hearing our good qualities

A full week together
Things gelling so well
Cooking, sharing, eating
Mindfully walking

Family games
Hiking and songs
Community letting go
into trusting practice

Kids feel the freedom
in their special programme
Pebble med, art, sharing
feeding pigs and running

Core staff so skilled
Holding it all together
with their steady practice
Phap Son's wise talks

Spiritual ancestors
invite the bell for me
Deep energy flows
into sound vibrations

Gratitude as we end
in concentric hugging circles
Children in the centre
surrounded by adults

Such warmth of love
Radiates for us all
With hearts so open
Sowing Seeds Together

26 August 2013

COFFEE BOOK BIRTH

Mid-east meal with friends
Them seeing our sweet babe
Book starting to grow strong
Spread, attract in world

Cooking with Bob
to celebrate book birth
Proof copies out
Publication process

Good feeling says friend
Yes, I can see it
Just letting it flow
beyond grasping for results

Still image is clear
People's History spreads out
Attraction brings orders
streaming back in

Opening to energy
Yes, we deserve it
Bob's efforts manifesting
for Press and himself

Allowing abundance
Letting go of fear
Trusting Kev, Helena
Enthusiastic publicists

Greater involvement
My early jump-start
Mixing ingredients
Cooking with Bob

28 August 2013

Touching Peace Syria
within to shine out
In time of war threat
stability most needed

Easy to get caught
in War hysteria
Fighting for, against
energy gets tangled

Breathing slow, easy
way past blame
Clarity of mind
Unconditional love

How can we best
help gassed children
Beyond more violence
Reconciliation

Bringing to Peace Talks
all parties involved
Recognising, respecting
everyone's right to live

Writing to MP
with understanding
Demonstrating together
Touching Peace Syria

30 August 2013

In MP's surprise vote
reason wins out on Syria
Stability of understanding
that violence merely breeds

Savouring being British
in victory of peace
Celebrating success
of parliamentary sanity

Relaxed by London fountains
Grandkids play in water
Family enjoying city beach
Talking, eating together

This safety and harmony
we want for own family
Sending out justice energy
for everybody to share

So pleased to have chosen
this North Sea island
for future generations
Savouring being British

JEWISH HISTORY, NEW YEAR

Watching Jewish History
with Sophie and Bob
She sits through with interest
being also her identity

Orthodox Haggadah
says each generation
tested with sorrows
God will redeem us

Woman at table says
always thought reality
to watch out for worst
coming from our history

I see where it's from
My dear Find The Worst
More than old brain
Flows from ancestry

God of sin, guilt
wrath, punishment
Apparent to me
believing out of fear

Yet ten commandments
also hold precepts
don't kill, steal, lie
no adultery, love neighbour

No need to reject
tablets wholesale
Take what is helpful
without God threats

I pour upon earth
worry/fear to transform
Compassion, solidity
Meditating with Buddha

Working with positive
best way round for me
Actions have consequences
We can learn and change

At end of programme
asked Sophie what thought
Good, I knocked on door
with Ella at Passover

They came in as the prophets
May all hungry join us
We'll invite her each Seder
Yes, Sophie wants to come

*   *   *

As Jewish New Year starts
at sundown tomorrow
I want to share sweet blessings
with loved-ones and friends

Shana Tova
Happy New Year
Jewish and school
Sunshine welcomes

Sitting by river
watching ease of flow
into five, seven, seven, four
May consciousness spread

We are the ones
who can make peace
Within and without
May harmony resonate

May we be healthy
happy, successful
in being the beauty
Shana Tova

**After seeing Schama's
Story of Jews 2**

Jewish Transformations
from despised wanderer
Stepping into freedom
Resonating right now

Vibration of bell
through generations
Who just *vant* I should be happy
And that's what I can do

Ancestors bloodied
oppressed and maligned
But we choose life
Savouring the beauty

In family warmth
we unfold anew
Strength and fortitude
Yiddisha Mamas

Choosing what to take
from sacred heritage
Passing on traditions
reflecting tolerance

In this New Year space
Compassion for all
Starting with myself
Temple discounted woman

No longer need to argue
Be 'other' within/without
This toxic mindset
I hold with understanding

Seeing the traps
of victim/oppressor
Not needing either
Dissolving dualism

Focus of kindness
allowing energy through
into gut of fear
Actually body powerhouse

Recognising belly
as my deep centre
Spreading and spreading
out to the Oneness

Back to Mother Earth
True Goddess tradition
Even God unnamed
is actually beyond gender

Seeing the contradictions
dialectical divisions
come together in clarity
past grasping to be right

Taking care anger
hurt and despair
Accepting, embracing
Jewish Transformations

16 September 2013

Twentieth Anniversary
of Cambridge Sangha
Meeting back at Mike's
where it all began

Still founder members
to pass on the history
Sharing with new friends
and children as well

Healing with Sangha
my deep heart rift
Twenty years of energy
building for us now

More than individuals
Collective Karma
available for each
Together more than sum

So many sittings
Such suffering transformed
Learning from other's insights
and difficulties overcome

Sharing my troubles
over so many years
Deep listening of friends
helped to sustain me

Focused in practice
Bell vibrates through
Walking, touching earth
tasting her bounty

In hugging meditation
our hearts meet again
Feeling connections
Intertwined growth

18 September 2013

Just let it all settle
and it'll work itself out
Bob says when we can't
get toner replacement right

Late into the night
after trying so much
Just leaving my printer
Red error message shining

Tired, I give up caring
knowing phone calls next day
In dreams of forcing things
I awake with discomfort

But it comes to me
maybe paper is stuck
I open tray to check
and find it is empty

Bursting into Bob's study
It's the paper!
He smiles, let's see
and I print a poem

As simple as that
There's a message for us
So wound up with Book Launch
Need to regain perspective

In twenty-one turnings
I see again so clearly
Beauty of family project
beyond promotion details

Bob so agrees with me
as we ready for holiday
The romance of our lives
A special time to savour

Reminds me of Victorian
book titles we sell
Initially Bob disappointed
not that many bought

Suddenly this summer
coming from nowhere
many orders appear
for the whole series

Somewhere on this planet
there's a summer course
or discussion on Internet
Way beyond our knowing

I want Bob to be satisfied
with his coffee book launch
He's put so much into it
and I have as well

And this is the lesson
of trying too hard
It'll work itself out
Just let it all settle

30 September – 4 October 2013

FIRST WEEK IN SALEMA

Salema in the rain
as never seen before
Cloud and coolness
Beauty of ocean

Slipping into being here
Rhythm of the waves
No hope of swimming
in this weather shift

Still we've arrived
Closeness together
Sharing the space
of leaving it all behind

Us refugees from beach
sheltering at Atlantico
Hot chocolate supersedes
usual ice cream

Mesmerised by the sea
even through rain drops
upon window glass
with warmth separation

Wonder of waves
in constant procession
Roar of the whiteness
breaking against sand

*   *   *

Reading at night
to Bob out loud
Anne of Green Gables
Mom's old favourite

All those children's classics
which I missed years ago
Downloaded for free
Seeing what Florence liked

Anne the optimist
with such imagination
If I'd liked to read then
could've enjoyed as kid

*   *   *

Savouring swim with Bob
Fully immersed
floating on turquoise
Enjoying the ride
over soft waves

Glowing with life
Smiling so wide
Such a deep pleasure
to be here with him
in my liquid home

Red rocks exposed
Layered ones in view
Slabs of vast time
puts all in proportion
Savouring swim with Bob

SALEMA WITH FRIENDS

Seeing old friends
dinners and chats
Catching up from last year's
reminiscent connections

Tineke and Don
building up their land
Art and excavation
Adding a new room

Isabelle and Dario
Him feeling better
Her Portuguese power
in action and kindness

Michael and Maureen
make us surprise dinner
St Ives paintings
their old van adventures

Jarvis and Virginia
He tells of her in China
Him still in fisher cottage
year round life in Salema

And what of us
melting into ease
as boats deposit fish
May they go to Pure Land

*   *   *

Watching the sea come up
from rock shade of last day
after warmed by music
Don, Tineke's trips, talks

Musicians' event
playing, singing together
Yoga teacher sells veg food
at San Migel family home

So many wondrous worlds
the tides and currents bring
Letting my heart unburden
from a deeper place

RETURNING FROM SALEMA

Flowing through currents
cold, warm with sun
in sea of life essence
and material world

After swimming expanse
in ocean so wide
returning to home
White sky, green land

Spending three weeks
watching the tides
Water softly darkens
sand to a brown

White waves upon
red rock and grey
Water erodes
time tablets so old

Centuries compressed
into coloured layers
falling once again
into bolder for shade

From there I can see
endless transformation
within and without
Flowing through currents

21 October 2013

Sister Kovida
Wandering nun
So glad to be with
her smile and wisdom

Coming back to teach
Vipassana insight
Sangha shares energy
in a mindfulness way

Receiving body
just as it is
Impulses and aches
Tripod solidity

Legs and buttocks
grounded to earth
From this base
backbone rises

Head on top
pulled up toward sky
by invisible thread
Stretching out spine

Beyond words
or watching breath
Direct experience
Choiceless awareness

Feeling so much
Enough to keep interest
Waves and twinges
moving through body

Ah, that's thinking
What is it like?
Angled whoosh
across my forehead

Worry planning
Sensing the grip
clutching heart
with being bad fear

Such compassion
naturally arising
for this Joy, trying
Trying too hard

Back to body
what a relief
Birdsong breaks through
Pleasant sound

Connecting with tension
build-up to release
Body vibrates
in letting go

23-26 October 2013

CRYSTAL HEALING

Working with Orange Calcite
Discover called Joy Stone
Bought from Mal in Market
Our friendship grows

Catching the light
Orange Calcite
Taking into Hara
expanding through body

Natural motion
No need to force
After cleansing
energy just flows

I am peace
deep in belly
Orange crystal
radiating out

Watching it happen
Being the witness
to thoughts and worries
which come and go

Opening to Oneness
there all the time
Being that wide
Catching the light

*   *   *

Orange Calcite
to right foot pain
Cool then warmth
Feeling the healing

*   *   *

Tangerine Quartz vibration
Splendorous life beauty
allowing clarity through
Releasing the heart

Heart Opening on Heart
allowing clarity through
Quarts crystal vibration
Splendorous beauty of life

Tree alight with orange leaves
Appreciation bursting out
Mom, Dad so loved these changes
Painting in nature while I played

Here I can be with them again
Allowing such orange in body
Feeling it's rich resonation
deep in Hara centre of being

What a wondrous moment
Now watching wave of fear
Compassion arises for you dear
Heart Opening on Heart

October 27, 2013

Book launch went so well
Culmination of Bob's creation

Family together
making it happen
Kids selling books
Kev, I manifesting

So many friends
come to celebrate
Enjoy presentation
Slides open worlds

Bob as fluent expert
From seed of Trieste
1950's beat café
Italians share warmth

In his exploration
discovering aspects
from slavery to revolution
Multinationals to Co-ops

Telling it with insight
from unique perspective
Researcher, creative writer
café, coffee lover

Black Apollo Press
Bob's brainchild
nearly twenty years on
Independent publisher

Coffee Book
older than that
Part of life's work
Accomplished so well

My dear Bobby
beloved life partner
So happy for us all
Book Launch Glow

29 October 2013

After Kev, Ella visit
quiet sit recovery
So happy to have them
Gladdening my heart

Sharing Florence with Ella
She thinks is nice name
With earnest wonder
says would've liked to met her

I explain that she does
through me and herself
Sewing and collage
Yes, Ella likes those too

Maybe that's where I got it
from my great grandma
Origami Peace Crane
passed down from Mom

Kevin cheerfully teaches
remembering once more
They colour them with love
for me to use at Transitions

My dear grown son
Your creativity grows
with Looking Machine
combining art and research

May your proposal flower
into funding this time
Or just do it anyway
Expressing your insights

1 November

Written for WYSING
Meditation teaching
and Reiki giving
for lovely artists

Mindfulness Meditation and Art
manifests in moment of peace
Alive in this energy of poem
Growing out of my practice

Walking upon the earth
feeling her beauty vibration
rising up with such power
Life Force of Mother Nature

Watching the sway of leaves
Deep green with intricate edges
Seeing clear, like when I draw
Three dimensional trunk

Pleasing to be in tree presence
Happy as sun streams through
Water ripples gently by
and I let myself just feel

No need to re-chew my suffering
Return to that cycle of regret
Noting its appearance, I smile
With kind observance, it passes

Watching the clouds do the same
White fluff across blue expanse
Never again, this special instant
Opening my heart to take it in

Little moments, glimpses
sometimes strung together
into space of such freedom
Mindfulness Meditation and Art

Life As Art
Art as practice
Interconnected
in being aware

Open to muse
within and without
Nature's beauty
Mind the painter

Yes, of course
sad scenes as well
With heart unlocked
compassion can shine

Aspiring to be
wide eyed seer
Sun when it comes
through passing clouds

Feeling the wonder
Vividness of clarity
Letting go distraction
to be with branches

Swaying and moving
in shades of green
Experiencing flow
Life As Art

Mindfulness as Protection
to allow sensitivity
without overwhelmed
or unbearably hurt

Better than alcohol
drugs or shutting down
Steady awareness
allows solid grounding

Staying in present
here in this body
Being projector screen
Watching movie upon it

Yes, it takes training
sensitive mind instrument
But that's what artists do
We work at our craft

Amazingly worthwhile
to practice awareness
Building balance, harmony
in sync with Mother Earth

Feeling feet upon her
Now sinking in deeper
Breathing her atmosphere
Mindfulness as Protection

*   *   *

3 November 2013

WYSING Wonder
Reiki and Event
Teaching Meditation
Reading my Poems

Branch cuttings come along
forming instillation
in gallery space
where audience enters

They become participants
in mindfulness miracle
Resonating with awareness
the energy grows

From breath watching
in sync with the bell
We gradually build
to longer guided sit

Then stepping into darkness
focusing on our feet
Touching Mother Earth
Wind whooshing us on

So happy to share
helpful practice for me
Welcoming new comers
into being so alive

So satisfied this morning
After 100 minutes
doing Reiki on artists
then public event

Explaining Judging Habit
What was that saying?
'Good I noticed'
Woman says will use it

Gareth says they liked it
in feedback forms
And he did too
We hug in friendship

Weaving mindfulness
into arts experience
Where it naturally belongs
in vivid zone of focus

*   *   *

Knocked over by waves
last night in the storm
of sleepless heart sorrow
with resources drained

Feeling the victim
Seeing the mindset
Knowing what it is
but swept up all the same

My normal buoyancy
allowing me to float
exhausted during day
Nothing left to sustain

Trying all the ways
to come to balance
brings some relief
But despair rushes back

Finally I get out of bed
to help break the cycle
of defensiveness, fear, anger
Slowly calming with the light

Eventually return to sleep
Waking so vulnerable
like an injured deer
Knowing the cause

My resources have limits
though I can stay calm
Result of day's depletion
Knocked over by waves

*   *   *

Sunlight this morning
out on the common
doing Chi Kung
to raise energy

Silence and sweet grass
sparkling with drops
of life essence liquid
as I sink slowly in

Just being the body
Eyes taking in brightness
Arms naturally flowing
with movement of legs

*   *   *

Replenishing heart
Rebuilding harmony
Reconnecting to positive
energy misplaced

Finding I'm still reeling
from other night's crash
Taking quiet time
to nourish sustenance

Re-establishing smile
from weakness place
where instability
returns old habits

Still there old friends
coming back to haunt
Beyond transformation
strong loops remain

Letting the Buddha
sit and breath for me
No one sitting
No self to suffer with

Returning, returning
to beauty of Green
Yellow leaves fall
as branches sway

Being three dimensional
again with the trees
Seeing how I'm human
with such vulnerability

No one to blame
Not even myself
If I wasn't thus
how could I understand

This is how some folks
feel all the time
After just one night
needing to refocus

Vietnamese people
caught up by typhoon
Awareness for you
Letting light through

I know I can do it
Practice brings trust
Just as before
Replenishing heart

*   *   *

Embracing wound
Feeling the lack
There such old yearning
to be loved as I am

Dear Mom and Dad
you did try your best
Each with limitations
transforming in your lives

I walk with you now
Sun streaming through
Our love resonates
supporting us all

So here we are
with autumn beauty
Bright splendour of leaves
then crunched underfoot

What else can I do
but grow through the pain
Yes, acceptance helps
Knowing it hurts

Surrounded by awareness
brings back perspective
Allowing kindness through
Softening my heart

16 November 2013

1 December 2013

Kevin turns thirty-six
with family surround
Artist exploring
creativity and intellect

His daughter so tall
we do Lego together
with father still enjoying
building connections

Laughing with Helena
now Dr Walsh
Living out their vision
for justice and art

Starting new direction
of Yoga and Palates
A chance to discover
through body and spirit

Him as guiding teacher
in second chance FE
Releasing limitations
Kevin turns thirty-six

*   *   *

When Bob was that age
son, Kev, was born
A year of change, power
is how he remembers it

And when I was thirty-six
we sold up in San Francisco
Travelled in the van
then moved to Cambridge

Family Chanukah
Accepting happiness
wellbeing together
our energy of love

Each one's input
in their own way
Adding to the mix
of our unique recipe

Sophie so grown up
wisely councils Ella
'Everyone's a little weird
in their own way'

The girls so joyful
hugging each other
The centre of holiday
they light *Menorah*

Their presents reflecting
directions of interests
Sophie wants books
Ella, football gear

Singing, playing *Dreidel*
Owning familiar holiday
past through generations
Family Chanukah

Allowing in happiness
Kevin rings enthusiastic
Supervisor likes proposal
for PhD funding re-try again

Helena found Ella a new bed
Of course, on Free Cycle
Probably picking up in taxi
Reorganising her room afresh

Dr Walsh is still job hunting
She keeps sending applications
though very little work out there
Not too discouraged, as activist

Reproductive Rights for Irish Women
Her great passion with friend Ann
Public talk she's organising
Kevin went to his union picket line

Bob sends ace Café journalists
Ella, Kevin to doughnut opening
Sophie shows all her first article
published in Here & Now Magazine

Coming together for Chanukah
such warm family celebration
Kerin takes responsibility
picking Stephanie up from hospital

Bob's started painting again
enjoying using other side of brain
Preparing for his brother's visit
Great for them to see each other

And I've bought macramé threads
to do some winter crafty things
Opening, expanding with Joy
Allowing in happiness

*   *   *

Bob and Barry reunited
Finding brothers anew
So heartening to watch
and join in as well

Barry's big laughter
filling the house
Playing with Sophie
Taking pictures galore

On his way to India
Massively enthusiastic
Giving time to reacquaint
with English family

Connecting with great nieces
not seen since babies
Getting to know
who they each are

My old college friend
SDS Agitproper
Our lives intertwined
So good to see you

Off with Bob on trains
to cafes, museums
Space to talk together
Bob and Barry reunited

*   *   *

Happy unbirthday
my dearest Bob
Book review appears
Writing validation

Your wondrous creations
manifest in many forms
resonating heart, mind
I love and respect you

20 November – 17 December 2013

WINTER LIGHT

Hail taps on window
opening my eyes
Flock of birds scatter
No, it's just leaves

Yesterday's yellow
tree top splendour
departs from branch
as wind blows new phase

Where will you land
nourishing the earth
Our dear mother
Solid upon you

*   *   *

Happy Earthling
sitting cross-legged
Aware of grounding
Source planet reality

Walking in sun
low in the sky
Brightness in eyes
so pleased to receive

Water alive
flowing river
Reaching deep inside
to softness of being

Sea gulls above
in blue streaky sky
Steamy breath
Happy Earthling

*   *   *

Sun and fresh air
Ancient prescription
for healing mild flu
with brightness of life

Puff-winged swan
glides on shining river
Ballet of the soul
played out before me

Bare trees stretch wide
welcoming blue sky
Light we've awaited
transforming rain and gloom

Feet slow connection
to earth so vibrant
Heart energised
by beauty digestion

After gentle days
of reading and rest
Recovery aided by
Sun and fresh air

19 December 2013

Wise Vietnamese nun
upstairs at Phung's house
As we sit in their temple
her presence so sweet

Unfettered consciousness
brings accepting warmth
Third eye widens, sees
deeper judging mind

In kind surround
of Sangha focus
Realising more clearly
Allowing for insight

In perspective of watching
landscape of mind
Deep layers of 'shoulds'
come to the surface

Why should I like you
so jealous, impure
Can't even stay focused
after all these years

My dear old habit
of Find The Worst
Superego friend
wanting to be good

Winning of love
if I could be perfect
Though parents did love me
so much in own ways

Skilful to discover
yet another layer
in kind acceptance
of Sangha meditation

Transformation of knots to beauty
Macrameing sorrows into kindness
Weaving the life force through
generations of fear constraints

Resonating with Mother Earth
allowing the Chi to ripple up
Wind to blow away my suffering
Awareness to take in wonder

Orange Calcite necklace
forms in soft concentration
where memories of love overspill
in Dad's gift of pearls to Mom

Feeling that essence with Bob
as we grow older with affection
Bringing us closer together
Transformation of knots to beauty

*   *   *

22 December 2013

Celebrating the Solstice with Sophie
Toasting with mango juice glasses
Coming of the light once again
Opening to enjoyment of expansion

Toasting our granddaughter, as well
Her so surprised that we do
Such a nice person growing up
with a strong sense of herself

Wondrous quality she's always had
good thing for her to keep balance
with buoyancy, acceptance, clarity
Desire to learn, explore and read

As we walk to buy books she tells
what she'll do when she grows up
How her writerly forest cottage'll be
Extra guests rooms, study, library

It will be a peaceful place she says
and, of course, sheep and her dog
Now she's with Brownies, Sea Cadets
Already going away on weekends

Reading Ann Frank again in bed
Hearing what Bob explains
Aspiring inventor soaks it all up
Celebrating the Solstice with Sophie

27 December 2013

BOXING DAY GATHERING

Family intertwined
from Kilmacow to Cambridge
London nexus
spreading through generations

Back to San Francisco
New York and Russia
All coming together
in living room celebration

Speaking to Tom, Joanne
of Helena's accomplishment
Pride glowing all round
of her PhD completed

Seeing her with parents
their link so strong
Caring and genetics
shine in their faces

Sophie and Ella
looking like sisters
Sharing special bond
friendship and secrets

Hugging dear Kevin
Speaking of yoga
Love flows in all directions
Family intertwined

30 December 2013 – 2 January 2014

Our Winter Light Dinner
Nice evening with friends
Bob and I dance together
before they all come

Sharing our food
Making connections
Hugs, chats and Reiki
Feeling ease of warmth

Finding Thay's New Year
sayings bursting through
New Year New Me
Joy within, Joy all round

Free to be True Self
in New Year New Me
Opening way out
Transforming habits

Old fear so warn
ready to let go
Happiness, peace
What we all need

Laughing at my image
of consuming cake world
What a relief
not taking seriously

Seeing through
Find The Worst Loop
Loosing it's power
in translucency

Wash through me, wind
I'm ready to release
Constraints on this body
Life's too good to miss

*   *   *

Meditating at Midnight
Start of the New Year
with Dearest Bob
Wondrous life partner

Us dancing to Miles Davis
Reading from our works
Texting the kids
Sharing through the years

May this be a good one
Healthy creative happiness
Recycling the sadness
back into living beauty

Love beyond words
Bond power between us
Pleasure being together
Bobby, my special one

*   *   *

Sangha New Year
Phung cooks us nurturing
We sit together
after Ancestor Address

Warmth of connection
Old friends reappear
Practice through the years
brings us steady growth

We speak of resolutions
Free to be true me
Letting go deeper
Sangha New Year

5 January 2014

Starlight and river
rising me above
illness morass
to higher plane

After days in bed
Bob, sun encourages
earth walk to water
Watching swift flow

Muddied with rain
Streaming toward sea
My Heart pumps loudly
Life carries on

I do the same
Only at slower pace
Releasing my worries
Watching my breath

Letting Loved-one go
The best I can
Trusting for us both
Starlight and river

6 January 2014

We're closing the bridge
says nice, young manager
It's inconvenient now
Better than collapsing later

Sure, but for so many people
who use that bridge to go to work
they'll have to trek to white one
for all the next ten weeks

A far trudge for pushchair mums
cyclists with heavy shopping
walkers in snow and rain
to reach Stourbridge Common

But we have to wrap bridge
to protect river below
from falling rust, lead paint
that we need to get rid of

Back home in the warmth
Wind pelts rain on my window
and I think of the workers
just starting this big job

It'll be hard for that crew
suspended over rushing Cam
Windswept and exposed
to freezing elements this winter

So I wish us all well
We'll see how it unfolds
When finished, said manager
it should look real nice

8 January 2014

Written for WYSING
Requested for booklet
asking same question
to all last year's artists

Where do I see me in 25 Years?
In trees on Stourbridge Common
Branch tips stretching out wide
Growing toward blue sky and white

Where do I see myself in 25 years?
In laughter of grown granddaughters
Love flowing through generations
In their work and ways of being

Where will I be in a 1/4 of a century?
Awake in the timeless whole
Imperfectly a part of Oneness
Resonating through source planet

Where would I be in 25 years?
On a rocker, aged 91
Living in harmony with nature
Softly breathing and smiling

Where do I see Joy in 25 years?
In consequences of my actions
In those I've affected
Nowhere and everywhere at once

25 - 29 January 2014

RATS

How to best protect
life, love and mind
Choices seem clear
but also confusing

Should we poison rats
in shed and composter
Right by front door
where they could get in

Allowing the council
to put down the poison
While boarding holes, hoping
they'll move and not eat it

Restless night wondering
have I done the right thing
Remembering clearing mess
and their danger to people

Health hazard to family
yet they're living creatures
That's why neighbour's waited
tearing down her old shed first

Just letting go
of too much excitement
of rats and relatives
now more resolved

Still last night in dreams
of us bringing in poison
meant for Rats under shed
And then would we eat it

Kept waking myself up
not wanting that to happen
Murray said even Plum Village
has had to use exterminator

Rats eating from compost
both here and there
Though rat's health hazard
excreted bacteria dies

Mother Soil transforms
as with my hurt today
Accepting, releasing
Earth walking on Green

*   *   *

After Pete Seeger's passing
from good life at 94
Recently he'd said
keep your sense of humour

Listening to Pete Seeger
with Kevin and Ella
Three generations
warmed by his music

Bob asks me to do it
when I'm in London
After we do the same
the evening before

Bob as young child
bounced on the knee
of dear old travellin' Pete
staying at his parent's house

Hugging with Kevin
feeling strength of his body
As we meet at the Tate
enjoy Paul Klee together

Hugging Ella later
after showing me drawings
Helena sends applications
Tasting pizza and their love

Around Sangha fire
warm sharing last night
Joint meditation grows
collective consciousness

Sun shining wide today
Vivid and thawing
With more rain tomorrow
touching Pure Land now

Like thrill of client saying
mindfulness stuff works
Feeding positive habits
Letting negative go

*   *   *

What a Reiki relief
with Pran Mudra help
further releasing
even into sleep

Finger touching Mudra
thumb, ring and pinkie
brings such ease
Stopping thinking

*   *   *

After meditation
open eyes to Dad's photo
seeing my reflexion
in this instant of notice

He did come to let go
of resentments and worry
And Mom into serenity
I can do the same

I'm going to Plum Village
to twenty-one day retreat
After wavering with concerns
got the last camping space

Didn't want to leave Bob
or have him feel abandoned
In confusion, unsatisfied
He thought I'd already booked

So many misperceptions
of what I 'should' do
Bob is so supportive
We'll travel together first

After such misgivings
False sense of responsibility
for family, Loved-one
Life takes its course

Conditions click into place
of how things can work
Me camping at New Hamlet
Good to have a change

Dear Lower Hamlet full
Them doing restorations
Shocked only one place left
at New Hamlet, so reserved

Yes, momentum is there
for me to go this way
First Bob, I to Paris
rather than separate trip

Excited, relieved, scared
Hope that they'll still have
a foam mattress for my tent
But somehow I'll work it out

As with Vietnam trip
I just have to go
Trusting myself, Sangha
I'm going to Plum Village

3 March 2014

Portrait of Joy
Bob's beautiful mirror
of fullness and wisdom
Naturally radiating

Feeling, being
person he sees
Richness of my life
in these Savour Years

Oh, so thankful
to share them with Bob
Enjoying the closeness
of bonding so long

Experiencing wisdom
in teaching my students
So much enjoyment
passing on what I've learnt

Appreciating myself
Receiving the sunlight
Swans fly overhead
Deep whooshing sound

Allowing spread
of wings as I breathe
in Reiki wonder
Zen way of life

Being the smile
here before my birth
Transforming ancestral
angst and despair

Using practice skills
in meetings, meditations
to enrich the Sangha
and my deep commitment

Enjoying such *Naches*
laughing with granddaughters
Accepting my blessings
flowing through generations

Savouring, savouring
this warmth of being
My birthday with Bob
Portrait of Joy

Breathing in well being
returning to inner care
After message of annoyance
at too many needing help

Only from this place
of Metta for me
Can therapeutic power
naturally shine out

Sister Kovida is right
that's the way to see
sudden negative thought
Feeling too many demands

From accepting the safety
Relaxed in caring place
for ReikiJoy healer
Vibration just ripples

So beautiful to share
Reiju and treatment
with dear Sister Kovida
Rejuvenation after travels

A blessing for me
Generosity comes round
Tender beauty in connection
with gentle, clear nun

Watching river ripple
as she takes in Reiju
Meditating in presence
Wondrous flow of life force

*   *   *

Relaxing, letting go
before family gathering
Want to be solid, centred
to enjoy gifts of love

Not to be thrown
by Loved-one's inability
to empathise very much
So focused on own needs

In meeting my needs
Pinkish-purple light
Soft green healing
Breathing in well being

*   *   *

Sophie playing on computer
Bob painting in study
Me seeing beyond worry
blessings of this moment

Accepting Kerin
from this safe place
Releasing into trust
Fulfilment accomplished

19 March 2014

***After science experiment
shows cosmic inflation
Multicoloured ripples
predicted by Einstein***

Echoes of growth
like cosmic inflation
Rippling through me
in so many directions

Echoes of annoyance
old habit suppressed
or allowed to run wild
Either way extreme

Echoes of knowing
the way of true balance
Harmony of awareness
Big enough to hold it all

Echoes of babyhood
kissy, kissy, boo boo
Mommy's affection
developing within me

Echoes of yucky
bits that are also me
And that's alright
I'm good enough as is

Echoes of acceptance
That isn't to say
I don't want to improve
But I'm already wondrous

Echoes of disappointment
for being so imperfect
The nature of being human
Having suffering to transform

Echoes of desire
not to have to suffer
Noticing on deep level
punishing me for doing so

Echoes of feeling
reactions in body
Seeing brings kindness
arising for this person

Echoes of compassion
Resource expanding
just like the universe
Spreading life force healing

MACRAME CRYSTAL NECKLACE

Weaving life strands
in creative designs
Changing patterns
with similar knots

Tangling, untangling
then weaving on
Enjoying the process
along with the product

Being the weaving
as well as the weaver
Ever-shifting conditions
only like this for an instant

Reiki light winds through
with shimmering strings
Feeling and being
many energy currents

Picking up old strands
Releasing distortion veil
Seeing them more clearly
beyond Judge discoloration

Noticing that fibres
of guilt, fear, regret
can stifle inventiveness
They pass to new variations

*   *   *

Unblocking cave chambers
In depths stalactites grow
Unseen in fear darkness
They sparkle in the light

Beyond undermine barriers
vast treasures so great
With spacious exploration
finding deeper habit roots

Freeing you, my father
as I do myself
Dearest inner angst
Watching, understanding

With warmth of root tea
Ancient crafts re-practiced
Courage to feel, know
Unblocking cave chambers

*   *   *

On balcony of converted church
up amongst the vaulting
We sit hand in hand
and I suddenly understand

We get this time together
a miracle, dream-come-true
In clarity of our deaths
I savour your touch

A feeling of heaven
with stain glass windows
This insight so clear
like seeing back in time

I admire your painting
You, my crystal macramé
Tasting sweetness through body
at Michaelhouse Cafe

28 April 28 2014

FANNIE PASSES AWAY

Barry emails to say
Fannie has pneumonia
May she go to the light
with ease and comfort

A part of nature
Fannie said she was
We walk on Common
beyond time and space

Eyes to white sky
then down to Poplars
Reflected in river's
varyed hues of green

Oh yes, you like bark
of London Plain tree
Beauty of its texture
so many shades of brown

Grasses grown high
also attract
Seeds of continuance
as we do with you

Horse Chestnut blossoms
Great-granddaughters enjoy
Generations of artists
in diverse forms

Mom and Dad join us
Don't be shy Ed
Your legacy lives on
A part of nature

8 May 2014

Fannie passes at 101
in peaceful ease, as hoped
Barry, Annie with her
Him gently stroking face
She lets go on last breath

What a wondrous life
Dear Fannie had
Vivid and intense
Mellowing in late years

Such zest of beauty
Sky, flower connections
Her long stream of art
Energy of expression

Champion for justice
Picket sign maker
Marcher, organiser
Power of her actions

Love for her family
taking care of grandkids
Ed in later years
Supporting Bob and I

Glad you are free, Fannie
your energy to flow anew
Changing and spreading
A part of nature, as you said

So much a part of us
family and friends
You influenced so many
continuing through generations

I feel you within me
See you in spring blossoms
Your artist eye sharpens mine
What a wondrous life

12 May 2014	13 May 2014

After family memorial
for our dear Fannie
Chaos and wonder
Love intertwined

Walking by river
where we set free
Fannie At The Helm
boat with our messages

Such mixed emotions
Intensity and flow
Life Force Energy
continuing down stream

As boat began to sink
Ella started getting upset
Sophie said, 'she's part of nature'
Which we all could accept

Reality of limits
of my form, capacity
Holding this angst
in such tender embrace

Yes, I can feel you
in silence of beauty
Green expansive being
Walking by river

Confusion and release
Just letting go in cavern
blocking my way home
in last night's dream

Suddenly in America
me saying I'm a foreigner
Now just like Virginia Woolf
No country, but whole world

This old perplexity
how to protect myself
Yes, it's the illusion
that there's a separate me

Familiar pain, angst
that I'm lost and alone
When out in the sunshine
I'm so a part of nature

Just what late Fannie said
what resonates so right
In Oneness of being
kind inclusion of fear

14 – 26 May 2014

MAY RICHNESS

In Pure Land of wild flowers
projects, worries subside
Shifting back and forth
as sun comes in and out

Vivid tiny worlds
expose the wonder
Cow Parsley blossoms
Fragrance of freshness

Textured Willow bark
Multi-shades of brown
I reach out and touch
joining her solidity

Savouring bird song
Spotting fledglings
Mother protects them
In Pure Land of wild flowers

*   *   *

Olivier and Bob
Connection so deep
Back through their lives
weaving spirit of '68

In US, France, UK
meeting and sharing
Catching up once again
Many things to speak of

Interested in each other's
writing and living
families and politics
Discussed on long walks

Seeing them together
I just have to smile
Sincerity of friendship
Olivier and Bob

After visiting Phuoc in hospital
recovering from stroke
Determined and aware
practicing best he can
I'm touched, inspired

Richness of life
Spread of emotions
Clarity of purpose
I see in Phuoc's eyes

Practice diverse
watching thoughts, feelings
Difficulties in illness
provide mud for lotus

Compassion, we both agree
important for ourselves
Helps with the fear and
Richness of life

16 – 25 May 2014

PLUM VILLAGE PREPARATION

Plum Village preparation
Putting up my tent
Resurrected in back garden

Hugging Bob inside it
Feeling he'll be with me
Bob hugs his blessings

Settling my affairs
especially in my head
Letting go to trust

Emailing with Sister
about staying extra day
Feeling resolution

In last night's dream
There with Tomato Soup
You see, it's fine, alright

*   *   *

Ride back from Plum Village
to the railway station
will somehow work out
as it's always done before

No need to struggle
to change to Lower Hamlet
Habit patterns draw me in
I see control illusion

Like wanting to save Loved-one
Way beyond my remit
I'm only one can heal
then naturally shines out

*   *   *

After days of detailed packing
preparing for Plum Village
Fun at neighbour's party
then fear returns at night

In restless sleep tangles
What else should I bring
to feel warm and secure?
Yes, Mind of Fulfilment
already accomplished

Leaving it to the Buddhas
this planning, fear, worry
Letting heart gently open
to beauty of this moment

Surrendering to the flow
of Plum Village adventure
To return with more to share
with family, friends, Sangha

Sitting with fingers poised
Allowing words through to keys
Bob making lunch after painting
Shades of green sway in wind

15 June 2014

Plum Village Presentation on 12th Mindfulness
Training as part of OI panel given in New Hamlet

Born right after Second World War
into Jewish American family
Holocaust lurked through my childhood
Images of emaciated Jews behind barbed wire

In formative judgements of 'good' and 'bad'
taught Germans who just stood by, watched
while Jews humiliated, shipped to Death Camps
These Germans, too, were responsible

Energy of dualistic thinking
such a key to promote more conflict
As scars of Holocaust survivors
created slogan of 'Never Again'

If there's only two possibilities
either 'oppressed' or 'oppressor'
then next time better 'oppressor'
Affected Israel's mindset toward Palestinians

This dualistic gut reaction
fuelled by such deep fear
Inherited from the Holocaust
was reborn in new generations

Begetting yet more violence
hatred, discrimination
Cycle feeding cycle
causes anguish for all sides

Like when Vietnam War started
I couldn't be responsible for genocide
I had to campaign against it
to stop the killing in our name

Anger was our fuel
It went well with youth
and simplistic ways of seeing
Either part of 'problem' or 'solution'

Later reading Thay's BEING PEACE
was such a revelation
He said can't have peace out there
without peace inside, between us

This we hadn't understood
and it made us sectarian
self-righteous and demanding
to change the world, right now!

Thay's practice changed my approach
like giving out anti-war leaflets
Offering each passer-by peace
You know, so many more took them

Peace-walking on demonstrations
No longer need to shout
Better resonate with the earth
beyond narrowness of 'us' and 'them'

New ways of peace education
with environmental Transitions group
Teaching atomic bomb peace crane history
while making origami with recycled paper

I've so needed this practice
to be steady through family storms
Gaining clearer vision, humility
The need for greater acceptance

Invaluable for family reconciliation
from place of not having to be right
Beyond the blinding of that habit
comes more desire to understand

So from this wider perspective
with less discrimination
It's easier to listen, hear others
and truly work for peace

22 June 2014

NEW HAMLET, PLUM VILLAGE

Feeling more at home with myself
Drifting in and out of dream sleep
On top of plum orchard
just seeing the landscape

Swaying gently with stillness
one day after retreat
A chance to non-think
in shade of natural flow

Ever-changing body, mind
connected to environment
Ants I've shared tent with
them outside, above

Inner coolness of white space
Clouds, trees give shelter
No need to fear
Being transformation

Ebb and flow
beyond distinction
of pairs of opposites
which birdsong doesn't need

Wide with green energy
sprouting forth from Earth
So safe with you, here
Just allowing life's course

The force of letting go
looses separation to hillside
Nothing left to run about
Feeling more at home with Non-self

24 June 2014

After return from Plum Village
Thay's wondrous talks
International disciples
hear, experience no death

True Joy expansions
in so many directions
Vibrating in, outward
with no need for self

Made of non-self elements
Earth, sun, water, air
Experiences, ancestors
come together with a name

Thank you Mom, Dad
for giving it to me
Your post-war hope
encouraging this volition

So much easier to soften
beyond fear of extinction
Continuations insight
lessens need for grasping guard

If nothing here to keep the same
(though won't be completely different)
Can relax into flow stream
Beauty of transformations

Releasing fear of death
gives me so much space
to open to natural glory
of creative abundance

Supporting Manas self-lover
to release 'How could I have
such negativity reflected upon me
When no one's here to defend

Beyond autonomous illusion
coming up to be discharged
Is great lesson, so helpful
Empty of Separate Self

Containing the Cosmos
This person called 'Joy'
Given conventional designation
but made of non-Joy elements

How would I know what'll happen
or what manifestations'll become
By nurturing positive seeds
future grows in that direction

May my thoughts, speech, action
pour beautifully into river
Continuing as ripple waves
with true base in water

*   *   *

Digesting experience
of Twenty One Day Retreat
Feeling Thay's transmission
through various meditations

Of course, not completely
Growing out of former one
Letting barriers disintegrate
Trusting that much

Sitting, last night, with Sangha
Giving them pine cones
brought back from going
as a river to Son Ha Temple

Here in this being
such beauty of peace
Nirvanaising each moment
the only time alive

Continuing vibration
Nurturing, enjoying
Mind Consciousness practice
understanding for Manas

This naturally supports
wholesome seed growth
Noticing, embracing negative
shrinking back to Store

Perfection of Store
without any effort
Harmony of seeds
Balance beyond judgement

Transformation at base
though Store, itself, a wonder
Releasing of dualisms
brings such freedom

Only through Manas
does judgement arise
In separate self illusion
distortions appear

Thay's Continuation Body
transmitted to me
from sitting, walking, listening
with Sangha, twenty one days

Dear Mind Consciousness
supporting practice
In lushness of summer
I return a different person

Returning home to live
way of Bodhisattva
Life after life
Manifestation only

28 June 2014

BASED ON THAY'S MINDFULNESS TALK

Mindfulness as the way
Much more than a tool
Each step and breath
can bring Nirvana
extinction of ill-being

The beauty of practice
right into daily life
No need for separation
of sitting meditation
All part of being alive

Only in this instant
can we wake up
Past already gone
Future hasn't happened yet
So blessed to have this Now

Beauty of nature
Mother Earth source
Life force so green
Budding leaf spreading
Sharing so wide

In this interconnection
breathing transformed oxygen
Conscious in, out of lungs
Continuing through body
Supporting each cell

Cells working together
with such cooperation
Inner/outer intermeshed
in Cosmic Body
Beyond dualism, perfection

In Deep Relaxation
with kind awareness
releasing body tension
Appreciating this marvel
keeping me alive

Heart pumping day, night
circulating freshness
So thankful to you
Do want to live right
to support wellbeing

Opening to restorative
sound of the bell
Vibration profound
Brings back to True Self
No need to run away

Kissing earth, each step
linked back to breath
Arrived, Home Now
Reverberating life force
Allowing healing through

Stopping and calming
in grace of this moment
Happiness more important
than power or wealth
Illusionary desires

Flowing with clarity
of ethical path
Three trainings base
Mindfulness, Concentration
Insight naturally arises

Nothing to run after
Everything's right here
This wondrous resonation
of spiritual energy
Mindfulness as the way

30 June 2014

Opening to Emptiness
a key to understanding
Learning the lessons
without needing such pain

Connecting Conventional
and Ultimate Dimensions
Emptiness makes Diagonal Zed
with Infinity Spin Perfection

Beyond need for pride
to balance inferiority
Complexes so tangled
rooted in hurt, fear

In just letting go
lushness of summer
Green growth so wide
frees up the spirit

As true Interbeing
with no real, separate self
No 'I' to defend
or shame to hide

Beyond judgement separation
There's nothing left to prove
Full sigh of relief
held in Nature's beauty

With energy of Insight
it's safe enough to trust
Allowing transformation
Becoming Emptiness

2 July 2014

REPORT ON 21 DAY RETREAT

What happens when we die?
Thay says short answer is
just that we don't
What happens when we're alive?

Nectar of Immortality
Eight Bodies, Thay teaches
So many continuations
while we're still breathing

Releasing to grace
of Ultimate Dimension
felt through these bodies
in interconnection

This Human one, so grateful
Want to treat you right
Eating what supports
living with health, ease

Need physical body
to become a Buddha
Transcending dualistic notions
like 'being' and 'non-being'

Buddha, Dharma, Sangha
Bodies within, without
Linked in with practice
of living the way

Body Out of Body
Nonlocal, everywhere
People Thay's never met
affected by his teachings

Like in Lotus Sutra
Buddha calling back
many Transformation Buddhas
from everywhere

Continuation Body
Cloud becomes rain
being both at once
As granddaughters and I

Our thoughts, speech, actions
are how we continue
Better future when they're beautiful
Can catch up, transform negative

No death, just continuation
Manifestations
In so many bodies
Compassion can heal

Cosmic Body
manifests from cosmos
Yet behind, a kind of energy
that you can't take out of cosmos

Phenomena Realm Domain
Object of our consciousness
Our body contains whole cosmos
with the Ultimate right in us

Cosmic True Nature Body
another name for Suchness
Reality itself
unfiltered by human perception

Deepest level of interconnection
of everything in the cosmos
Cosmic Consciousness
Could say this is the subject

But subject, object manifest togethe
Can't take object out of subject
Nor our consciousness from the sta
Leaning on each other in Perfection

And that is true base reality
Store Consciousness can touch
Beyond any judgement
seeds in interbeing as a wonder

From Life Force Mental Formation
Comes Manas - will to live
And with it grasping illusion
that body, skandhas are 'me', 'mine'

Pleasure seeking Manas
(somewhat like the Id)
views through good or bad for 'me'
The Lover's suffering aversion

Giving rise to Mind Consciousness
(Could be likened to Superego)
With appropriate attention practice
comes non-discrimination wisdom

No need to suppress Manas
but shining light upon her
brings awareness as best protection
No separate self insight

With eyes of Signlessness
beyond appearance or form
Seeing eight bodies manifest
way past birth and death

As water's basis of each wave
Ocean spreads in many ways
Water vapour back to clouds
Raining life for us all

Living in Mindfulness
as a way, not mere tool
Inseparable for wellbeing
from Eightfold Path

Interbeing with Right View
so our happiness depends
on way of seeing/acting
Practicing Mindful Trainings

Nirvanaising each step
Healing is the way
on transformation path
Life after life

10 July 2014

Bell of Mindfulness Instructions for MINDFULNESS FOR REIKI CD developing with new course manifesting from retreat

A Bell of Mindful
can bring us back
to the present moment
The only alive moment

The past is gone
Future, hasn't happened yet
Life is right now
No matter what our thoughts tell us

Our body stays here
though mind wanders so
Coming back together
We can resonate with Reiki

Our breath is the link
between body and mind
When we return to our body
life force can align

The bell is a reminder
It's vibration a call
Feeling it within
Coming back to breathing

This wondrous inner anchor
Taking in, allowing freshness
to be drawn down to belly
Deep within our essence

Letting go, releasing air
and muscle tension too
Softly floating out
into transformation

Let's just try it once
No pressure, see how it goes
The mind may naturally wander
just gently return to your breath

If it feels right
you can say to yourself
'In' on the inhalation
and 'Out' on the exhalation

(ONE BELL)

Now each time the bell sounds
taking Three conscious breaths
Not forced, just normal intake
Watching, being with breathing

And when the mind drifts off
If it feels right, you can say
'Good, I noticed'
Coming back, beyond judgement

Let's try Three breaths with the bell
Just using kind awareness
of our life-giving stream
through body, mind in Oneness

(BELL)

Let's offer ourselves the space
of Three bells, Nine breaths
May Reiki flow through breathing
down to grounding Hara belly

(THREE BELLS)

This reunifying way
is here for us any time
With our own bell or life's noises
There's lots of potential reminders

Even ringing of our phone
can be used in this way
Breathing through three sounds
We're more relaxed to truly live

15 July 2014

THE BUILD BEGINS

I see you there Manas
grasping 'I want
buildings my way'
Getting caught up

Yet beyond
three year old mentality
I know I already have
enough to be happy

And the thing is
that I often am
But again entangled
in neighbour's projects

Reacting to his plans
Architectural drawings
Noise, disruption to come
what we can do on our side

Causing stress
for Bob and I
We loose perspective
and begin to argue

Yes, we go for walk
Talk it through once more
Our good intensions
bring us back to awareness

Although recycled conservatory
would be a nice addition
I could get winter light
in many other ways

Just letting it go
so things take their course
Calming needy illusion
I see you there Manas

20 July & 15 August 2014

Amazing agreement
to move Conservatory
from next door to here

Connecting with a builder
that I now need to trust
We will pay him ourselves

Sister free from cancer
Strengthening our bond
of long love beauty

Preparing for the Retreat
So glad Sophie's coming too
But need to organise, pack

A lot on my plate
but all the way it's looked at
as this is what I wanted

* * *

Conservatory deconstruction
Ian whistles while placing sections
throughout our back garden
as neighbour's building work starts

Their triple house extension
Deafening demolition hammer
This summer's reality
with challenges, we hope rewards

As our carport's in construction zone
we'll work for rebuild as studio
Separate space for Bob to paint
and have special place out of house

22 July & 10 August 2014

Accepting Loved-one
just the way she is
with High Function Autism
and emerging Higher Self

With perceptual difficulties
experiencing life uniquely
What I can do to help us
is release my regrets

Though I know it's true
on level so profound
not always easy to realise
she's best daughter for me

So motivated to deepen
on my spiritual path
from relationship with Loved-one
For this I have to thank you

Of course, none of us wanted
the hell we've all been through
But for this lifetime
you are my best daughter

As this insight emerges
I feel my resistance
as didn't want such suffering
Though this is its transformation

Clarity no reflection
on me, as no self
and cause and effect
inter-are anyway

I can more easily
accept bounty flowering
of lotus from mud Now
beyond future expectations

May this sparkling energy
spread to dear daughter
as she explores own goodness
and inner light of love

Loved-one's shifting fruitfully
Doing positive meditations
Seeing herself as
light worker with gold hallow

May love spread between us
and throughout the family
Accepting special needs
and true person beyond them

*   *   *

Family Retreat warmth
Opening to Loved-one
with own operating system
Seen through Sangha eyes

Watching her connection
to so many adults
Children as well
feel her special quality

Under less pressure
with practice surround
She can join in
in ways she best can

23 July 2014

Introduction to poems I read about looking at landscape from different angles for Family Retreat Workshop

The analogy of seeing
the mind and surroundings
as landscape helps bring kindness
to negative, thoughts, feelings

It's aided me accepting them
with greater perspective
Stepping back appreciating
the energies that make 'Joy'

Enjoying the landscape
within and without
Beyond separation
interwoven as one

Watching the vista
of scurrying mind
onto this, then that
grasping for satisfaction

Took a while to notice
what's below impatience
Been running away
Finally stopped to breathe

What a *Mahiya*
that calming effect
Discovering and holding
the fear coming up

Suppose it's these sufferings
(much less than before)
that remind me to savour
the wonder of awareness

Seeing's so helpful
bringing understanding
Compassion arises
softening the heart

Choices of focus
so many, varied
Choosing to breathe
through lungs down to feet

Solidity reassurance
Wider picture emerging
The beauty of river
gently flowing on

All I have to do
this very instant
is feel each step
Heel, soul on source planet

From there surroundings
bringing such comfort
Wide tree roots down
grounding back to earth

I hold tree in my arms
bark against my cheek
Forgetting my worries
in your peaceful strength

25 July 2014

During Gaza War
sending love, support
to Peace Group friends
met in Plum Village

Walking by English river
with no incoming fire
I hold all your hands
letting comfort ripple out

Our Sangha sits with them all
Palestinians and Israelis
Breathing, rippling out
our energy of peace, solidity

May understanding
rain down, replacing missiles
Fear and hatred soften
to allow for just peace

They reply will send out
our message to Sanghas
Please stay connected
keep sending healing energy

I know we are all
really the same peoples
Down deep we just want
to live happily in harmony

Compassion for Middle East
war zones exploding
Children of Gaza
Palestinians, Israelis

May that true energy
radiate outward
in all directions
Ceasing hostilities

Dear friends on all sides
working for peace
In this hellish time
I send love, support

21 August 2014

Quietly home alone savouring the peace and gentle garden
digging for our recycled conservatory moving closer to reality

Wide brush strokes
of cotton clouds
outside my window
Sun peaking through
as I luxuriate in bed

In the back garden
they're digging the base
for our recycled conservatory
Now in bits, strapped to tress
Leaning against wooden table

As conservatory moves
toward re-assemblance
to manifest anew
on our side of fence
taken down for build

I'm happily hopeful
while still accepting process
But underneath a glimmer
that protected winter light
could shine through for us

All week I've been driven out
by noise of jack hammering
and vibrations of machinery
from neighbour's build
Now it's quietly our turn

Somehow they're digging by hand
So I'm enjoying this wondrous space
which I've been longing for
while taking refuge in UL, cafes
This - A peaceful time to just rest

Yes, I appreciate those outer places
But after two fantastic retreats
with a catch-up and pack month between
What I've been missing, I'm savouring now
Home alone with nothing to do but enjoy

28 August 2014

Awareness of sound
Cracking on recording
Clicking of my mouth
Need to redo CD with Kev

Awareness of sound
Banging of builders
Churning cement mixer
Their rock music below

Awareness of sound
in UL tearoom
Clinking of dishes
Chatting and fan

Awareness of sound
and desire for silence
Awakening early
to meditate in peace

Awareness of sound
Granddaughter laughing
yesterday in London
Us catching up with speech

Awareness of sound
surround as I write
Seeking stillness in movement
and patience in life's delays

Awareness of sounds
Pleasant and unpleasant
Vibrating in my head
Breathing and smiling

Awareness of transformation
Widening and Reframing
Beyond 'shoulds' of time
Into open space of Oneness

30 August 2014

Aware of frustration
prickly and anxious
Held in soft embrace
of pink cloud of love

Angst from many sources
Our base no further along
House building site surround
CD needing rerecording

Kerin rang in night
having trouble breathing
A & E says it's OK
I just keep practicing

Still it's ganging up
so many things at once
Seeing expectations
Releasing best I can

Soon off to doctor
to say meds didn't work
This time I hope she'll
send me to dermatologist

All of this in proportion
of beauty of late summer
Bob and my loving bond
Seeing what's important

Holding with tenderness
the rawness inside
Understanding
Aware of frustration

6 September 2014

Recycling vibrations
Matt breaking up
bricks that stood for years
as wall of carport

We'll have that rubble
John had told him
for hardcore under
Joy's Conservatory

So this pounding noise
is true transformation
With cooperation
our light space is growing

Yes, there's frustration
disturbance, annoyance
Me shaken out of patterns
I think that I need

Quiet mornings to meditate
then write in the stillness
of silent revelations
coming up through mind

Awakening earlier
for noiseless meditation
Then working round
however day unfolds

Of course I have disruption
to shake loose old reactions
Entrenched perceptions
of how things ought'a be

Recently I hear you
quite often old friend
defiance, as protection
Not really useful

Nowadays I've better ways
to deal with feeling threatened
like holding it with compassion
Far more beneficial

But that takes noticing
frustration feeding more
Judgement once again
as I go round the circle

This is the problem
not the negative thoughts
which naturally spring up
from seeds in Store

It's not what happens
but how you deal with it,
Mom used to say
with common sense wisdom

Seeing the difference
in my feelings about
recycling noise here
and pounding next door

If brick wall neighbour building
on the edge of our garden
wasn't going to be there
neither would Conservatory

So it's one project
profiting us all
Beyond worry, resistance
just letting it happen

Feeding positive vision
beyond discrimination
of what I 'shouldn't' feel
Allowing greater acceptance

12 September 2014

Allowing heart to reopen
after scaffolding fiasco
Putting up without permission
across windows in our garden

Having to be assertive
Not so close to conservatory
need room to construct it
No poles by our front door

Having to compromise
the way of these things
But good studio estimate
No time to talk with Bob

Us passing in the night
Him back from Liverpool
Glad it was a good trip
I leave early for London

Letting go of tension
giving Reiki, meditating
Preparing to redo CD
Accepting whatever happens

Warmed by being with Kev
Helena and later Ella
Their energy so buoyant
Helping me to soften

Setting up equipment
in Ella's room
The quietest place
in their lovely, small flat

After numerous glitches
Stops for random noises
We record half of CD
before banging intensifies

Accepting impossible
to go on that day
Picking Ella up from school
So wondrous to see her

Off to Hackney Farm
Ice Cream, coffee, cake
Making Cards together
for Helena's birthday

Great to draw with Ella
as Kev and I used to do
Then she shows me her guitar
Helena got through Free Cycle

I teach her to sing
Where Have All The Flowers Gone
With Ella's long hair
I'm reminded of Joan Baez

Kev finds Joan singing that
back in 60s on Internet
I sit close to Ella
We practice it together

Explaining it's a peace song
Ella looks deep in my eyes
'When will they ever learn
it's better to live in harmony?'

I come home to do that
Accepting my blessings
beyond building intrusions
Sweet life with Bob

When conditions are right
Conservatory and studio
will manifest with CD
Now keeping heart open

13 - 15 September 2014

SEPTEMBER RECYCLING

Ploughing Mind fields
Releasing tense weeds
Planting positive seeds
Nurturing to flower

Fertilising with beauty
of nature's river flow
Swans gliding through
Gray babes with mum

Waters reflecting green
leaves stretching out
seeking the sun's
transformative force

Watching from bank
seeing life unfold
Heron on other shore
Suddenly in flight

Opening to being
this moment as it soars
above high grass field
Disappearing as it lands

Held in sweet awareness
worry naturally untangles
subsiding into Oneness
Ploughing Mind fields

*   *   *

Reset to True
default nature
After Reiki treatment
by Liz and Rahelly

Them listening first
to all of my woes
Building noise, disruption
Loved-one difficulties

What spiritual friends
I am so grateful
Years of us practicing
loving way together

Each one benefiting
Returning back home
to energy of harmony
Reset to True

*   *   *

Waiting for builders
in so many ways
Arriving, constructing
recycled conservatory

Sending out Reiki
for bits in our garden
to reunite in harmony
as place of light and beauty

Ian finally arrives
I tell him I'm sure
he'll whistle it back together
He laughs and jokes

There in the garden
I hear his wondrous whistle
Now that base is solid
recreation continues

I see my perspective
on studio negotiations
shifting back and forth from
Manas to Mind Consciousness

May I keep practicing
truly being assertive
from place of awareness
Beyond waiting for builders

PORTUGAL POEMS

In Lisbon park by mosque
Such closeness with Bob
Tenderness suspending time
after chaos and confusion

Feeling hurt and upset
from early morning rise
Followed by missing train
though waiting on right platform

Energy not there
for us to get on train
and understand though for Faro
it's one to take for Tunis

Back down to ticket sales
who sent us up to there
Language miscommunication
leaves us all in a state

Bob and I sit outside on steps
past our defensiveness
Making efforts to settle
then talk things through

As emotions calm
Bob brings us back to essence
Building energy of our love
Kissing, rubbing cheeks

Just as mosque was transformed
to bull ring then shopping centre
We change back into true selves
and wait for afternoon train

          *   *   *

How we get to Salema
which does feel like magic
Was opening our hearts to love
so that trust could flourish
and letting go of expectations

Through kindness of strangers
who suddenly offer us a ride
from Tunis right to village
Which we gratefully accept
and find ourselves in Heaven

          *   *   *

Orange sun breaking clouds
Swifts filling sky
Flying in all directions
as fog drifts across hills

And I am really here
Sound of surf in ears
whooshing like in, out breath
Beyond needing crutch of plans

          *   *   *

Streams of emptiness
Slicing layered time
sandy, brown cliff cakes
Cut through with red

Rich earth so fertile
Reaching back millennia
To dinosaur feet moments
implanted here so solid

Ocean roars behind
rock providing shade
Wind cools sun's heat
and I just let go

          *   *   *

Looks like Nirvana
Passer-by comments
In shade of Boia Bar
enjoying ice cream

Thanks for reminder
supporting deeper vision
White capped waves rolling
across turquoise sea

Inviting Mom to lick with me
and Dad to enjoy tropics
Soaking in the wonder
of being in Nirvana

*   *   *

Ancient young rivers
Repositioned by earthquake
Tides, sea erosion

Platelets of time
Cut through, then moved
into vertical cliffs

And here I sit in shade
Giving Reiki to Isabelle
Allowing energy through

Shifting, transforming
Life force re-emerging
Ancient young rivers

*   *   *

Dog lying in road
as some do here
Not hearing car
which doesn't see it

Dog run over
Me, giving Reiki
Life force soothing
Eternal flow

So many beach footsteps
Sea will wash away
These feet's impressions
and deeper resonation

Timeless Compassion
in unity of chant
Pure Buddha Nature
connection in us all

Way past reason
Owner, driver's story
The dog's or my own
Not being caught

In loving detachment
seeing beyond illusion
of these physical plays
to spiritual energy

Allowing wonder through
beyond seeking answers
Simply being Bodhisattva
And the dog does survive

BUILDING CONTINUES

Awoken by Manas
rousing me from sleep
Mind Consciousness pleads
but Manas insists not safe

Slowly I rise
into wakeful state
Fear shaking me up
Best tool of The Lover

Awake then for hours
Seeing this old habit
Afraid of death's similarity
to loosing control when asleep

Telling that I won't die
but just a part of change
Still Manas grasps
The squeeze is so real

Childhood anxiety
maybe goes back further
This ancient death terror
somehow linked with sleep

Sending Reiki to source
way past my knowing
Intoning chants to Oneness
healing everywhere, beyond time

Kindness I offer
this morning in meditation
to Manas fear monger
Well meaning though misplaced

Sawing next door
Banging of building
mixed with Dali Lama chant
Allowing heart to open

Sun breaking through clouds
Drying yesterday's cement for post
we used to fix our fence
While Matt builds Bob's studio

Laying laminate with Bob
Stopping, talking it through
Each with defensiveness
but pooling our energies

*   *   *

Awakened by drilling
hammering and sawing
Workers shouting, pounding
Loud building will pass

Bob's art studio roof
put together today
They work longer hours
We hope build's nearly done

Conservatory quietest place
Bob and I enjoy together
With our flooring down
light, heat coming through

*   *   *

Neighbours have decamped
Not capable of supporting us
leaving us with their builders
to deal with difficulties on our own

Disappointed, as they were friends
But they've cut themselves off
Their extensions bring us problems
Different workers here all day

Dealing with our anger
frustration and headaches
So transformation can occur
blooming into new era

Named Light And Beauty
Conservatory that we paid
to have moved to our side
is such a wondrous addition

Sitting in Light and Beauty
Resonating with Earth solidity
Drilling, pounding noises
but quieter than in study

Grateful for meditation
this morning in silence
before construction started
Allowing me to settle peacefully

Finding ways through
disruption, resentment
disappointment with neighbours
Assertiveness, balance

Never knowing what moment
there'll be sudden piercing volume
When I'll need to speak to builders
if things get over the top

I wish them well with roofing
May Bob's studio be waterproof
Adjoining neighbour's extension
Massive, slightly blocks our light

And I wish neighbours well
though they haven't supported us
as they said they would do
But I don't want to be entangled

Free and clear in Meditation
Tea connection to clouds
wondrous natural light
in conservatory we saved

Sue says taken advantage of
Depended too much on friendship
Neighbours want what they want
Their vision blinkers them to others

Could've had Party Wall Surveyor
to negotiate for our interests
Bob says that causes antagonism
And it's too late to do it now

At least I've had a chance to write
before noise drives me out
Headache making after awhile
though lovely in Light and Beauty

*   *   *

Healing the inner crack
symbolised by party wall crack
Schism widened by drilling vibrations
Feel victimised by 'trusted' neighbours

When I showed him wall crack
on his brief visit here
not able to be concerned for us
Just said we could paint over it

I'm left with this difficult reality
while Kevin, Ella are on train here
and Sophie, Kerin are coming
Want heart opened to enjoy family

So I chant to Avalokiteshvara
Ask Reiki to heal conflict source
Use Compassionate Detachment
to see, fill my crack with kindness

Granddaughters' laughter
still echoing in Light and Beauty
Conservatory window mist
decorated by their drawings

Their connection so strong
Family bonding so deep
Our weekend together
helpful for us all

Such a relief to find
all OK in own way
Brightness streaming through
dense cloud cover

Each with own challenges
It's the way you look at things
Kev advises, straight from Mom
Allowing me to see more clearly

What's this really about, he thinks
then deals with it from there
Healing, restoring balance
is essence of what I need do

Stiff neck as demonstrator
of victim mode consequences
Reawakened by life's beauty
Granddaughter's laughter
*   *   *
Learning from Sophie
Flexibility, acceptance
of sudden changes
not going as desired

Learning from Sophie
Find happiness other ways
Not stuck in disappointments
Move on, just laugh now

Mindful self-defence
a complicated balance
with strange men banging on roof
overlooking our kitchen window

Mindful self-defence
a challenging practice
From childhood not easy
to take care of myself

Mindful self-defence
with narrow tipping point
between passive and aggressive
Seeking middle way of assertive

Mindful self-defence
seeing neighbour defensive
Locked in his hard shell
not able to care, support us

His builder's young son
inconsiderate, disrespectful
Not covering mural, when asked
Putting scaffolding on our shed

Coming down for breakfast
find strange men standing on it
So difficult, invasive
but calmly talk to roofers

Carefully writing neighbour
still decamped with wife
Bob texts him as well
He just fobs us off

Sophie wakes, wants to play
Men put ladders against our house
climb, bang right by window
But Soph and I keep laughing

Finding resolutions
and IKEA flat packs
After hellish drive there
brings perspective to difficulties

Confusion in childhood
from when scapegoated
Legacy hard to break through
to clarity of skilful way

Manas misperception
of what is self-protection
Creating separation illusion
fuelling fear of mistreatment

Liz is certainly right
lots to learn from difficulty
To be able to act wisely
without carrying it with me

Letting 'self' down
if don't defend
Spinning mind arguments
Creating inner angst

The more I can untangle
twines of misperceptions
the easier to be assertive
in a true way

Reality of builders
who are inconsiderate
and neighbour as well
Feed this old reaction

So much annoyance
frustration and anger
Justified in unfair treatment
but still not helpful

Back to how's best
to truly be assertive
without aggravation
Mindfully watching

Responsible for my own actions
others' deeds bring them effects
I send them good wishes
and open to the Ultimate

Awareness so helpful
unearthing old assumption
must follow Manas' advice
or I'll be taken advantage of

Here in this present
vastness of life's beauty
There is no future
to be used by Manas

12 - 14 November 2014

Transformation light
in conservatory whiteness
of cloud cover glow
in new day alive

Wind and drizzle
Returning sea gulls soar
Transcending problems
of yesterday's build

Banging till 7 pm
two hours beyond limit
of legal acceptance
Eleven hours of disruption

My message has no effect
nor Bob's email
Finally Bob texts neighbour
He apologises and stops them

Drive, desire of building
walls of extensions
reinforced defensiveness
He lost empathy, perspective

He returns today
and she end of week
Hopefully this will help
and build will end soon

Bob's studio left for last
Hard to set met with Nick
But clearly what's helping
is my transformation

Yesterday oiling new chairs
with mindfulness and Reiki
Beyond anger at builder's son
I speak to him through open fence

After rehearsal of angry way
this is so much better
Maintaining humanity
he finally apologises

Wood overhanging scaffolding
I've worried about in wind
is taken away by him
and says will cover mural

Whether or not he does
or asks permission to stand on shed
At least I made my point clear
while being respectful to us both

This is what I can do
keep my heart opened
Allowing healing through
Transformation light

*   *   *

Thay's illness brings reality
of what's really important
Stepping back once again
to imperative of awakening

Both to send him energy
and to live as his disciple
Being the rain of his cloud
falling on conservatory roof

Practice of drinking cloud
Thay's birthday gift to us both
Tasting moisture in my mouth
Swallowing, it becomes this body

Not separate from water
when I'm so made up of it
Very existence of this person
Reality of nectar nurturing

Mindfulness for Reiki Course
I've been preparing
over last five months
is successfully run

Culmination
of Thay's retreat insight
My course rippling out
from pebble he dropped

Waters running still
wavy and muddy
Learning from it all
to pass mindfulness on

Such a relief
and blessing too
Sitting with students
walking and eating

They gain from day
It helping us all
connect with Reiki way
of no separate self

Energy flowing
through body and mind
Sending to Thay
breathing in hospital

Thay so very ill
Sending him energy
Feeling him within
we just have to smile

His words coming back
Nowhere to go, come from
With my thoughts quieting
vibration of peace

Transformation at base
Perfect in wholeness
Learning through teaching
and creating materials

So here is my offering
to you my dear teacher
Breathing and smiling
Culmination

*   *   *

Blessed with what is
Meditating to Dali Lama chants
punctuated by drilling, banging
coming through party wall
Hearing as part of music

Releasing resistance
back to things as they are
Thankful electrician came
to liven Bob's Studio
with electric light, heat

After Bob's taping, priming
getting out builder's storage
Bob decorating Studio
transforming his hurt, anger
So pleased for him to have space

*   *   *

Unpredictability of build
never knowing about noise
Still drilling into party wall
Had to cancel client today

Accepting the reality
as Mom would say
Working with challenges
returning to blessings

Kerin goes to look at flat
offered her in London
Determined to do exchange
she's off to see it with Kev

Lovely time with Sophie
now in secondary school
Her sharing experiences
Trusting us with them

Growing up quickly
Loving reading, writing
Connections with Bob and I
She says kindness most important

*　　　*　　　*

Kerin and Kev see her flat
approve it's a good one
She wants a fresh start
May it go well for her

Had lovely Reiki Share
only half the students came
Accepting perfect numbers
Enjoying energy together

Banging now starts
I smile and breathe
Sending energy to Thay
feeling wonder of his presence

*　　　*　　　*

Bob's Birthday shifts
Him working in studio
Says it's my birthday present
Makes me feel so good

Him taking control
building book case
Me able to meditate
with mild banging/drilling

Taking back focus
to body and breath
Away from neighbour's
world of builders galore

Being Thay's disciple
the best that I can
Sending him energy
for transformation

Emailing Reiki students
smiling to our connections
Preparing for new term
integrating mindfulness

Allowing me to be
Reiki Master I am
for clients and students
for this person called Joy

*　　　*　　　*

Awakened Saturday 8 am
by hammering next door
loud against party wall
Can't meditate, write in study

Gone on for four months
six days a week
Really have had
more than enough of it

*　　　*　　　*

Just such a pleasure
to see Bob painting
in warm, light studio
Big smile on his face

19 – 25 December 2014

Family starts to gather
for Chanukah together
our annual celebration
of being Jewish love
Light at solstice time

Roses and laughter
granddaughters reconnect
as if never apart
Back to Harry Potter
drawing and talking
Creative pretending

Such wondrous energy
Kevin hugs me warmly
Bob cooking, sharing
difficulties of invasion
of builders who trample
without warning or asking

Kev makes up funny scenario
Theatre Arts group
climb on neighbour's roof
suddenly perform by them
But this is just a free space
for us to do what we want

Turning it all round
when there's some banging
Girls in Holiday Room
suddenly bang back, giggle
Our house 'reconfigured'
with happiness together

*   *   *

Transformation toward the light
as earth tilts in that direction
Quiet descends on house
with builders gone for now

At wondrous Chanukah
girls even write poems
Light candles on their own
Share secrets in the park

Working through challenges
of Loved-one under stress
Everyone making efforts
to enjoy family time together

Bob's toothache subsiding
Me feeling ancestors through
continuation of Jewish Culture
passed to new generations

Kevin doing so well
on PhD and teaching
Helena finally getting work
Doing performance art protest

Allowing shift through
stiffness in neck, shoulder
Day of Mindfulness warmth
working with difficulties

*   *   *

So many lilies gathered
from mural Bob painted
Black-haired woman reaps

From this wide place
all is very well
Enjoying Christmas peace

2 January 2015

THAY

One penetrating all, all penetrating one
Thay within, sending him energy
Feeling reverberation, I smile

Continuations, Interbeings
Birdsong vibrates through body
Husband, granddaughter's voices drift in

And here I sit, fingers on the keys
Digesting bagel, soya cream cheese
Old tastes in new forms

Thay, I feel you a part of me
Sending Reiki for transformations
whatever forms that takes

Your teachings come back to me
through your words and actions
Struck by how you erased the board

In those days I still did the same
with my refugee students
But after seeing you, became a practice

Now it's morphing and deepening
in our post haemorrhage relationship
Powerful energy interconnections

And my New Year's resolution
Beautiful, Compassionate Transformation
at Store Consciousness Base

Our energies support each other
in fresh ways of evolving
One penetrating all, all penetrating one

5 January 2015

Rediscovering old reflections
Cards picked at Thay's retreat
When he could teach with speech
and I brought much younger Sophie

I guess one was for each of us
but I've ended up with both cards
in a bag with the Two Promises
Stuff to show Soph when time's right

One's about transforming suffering
by sitting and gaining insight
That s/he who made you suffer
did so out of their own suffering

With only mild building noises
and two weeks of healing quiet
I can see that with neighbours
Transforming my anger/pain

That brings me to second card
Meditation on Love
With it in your heart
every thought, deed can bring a miracle

Keeping my heart opened
in a larger non-self way
Surely best way to talk to Loved-one
about effects of her social difficulties

Breathing as world restarts
in 2015 fresh way
After dream we were moving round
appreciating our stable house

So thankful Thay's recovering
whatever form that takes
Careful not to try too hard
Sending energy when it's right

Stay with Heron beauty force
rather than builder's noise
Family complications
best dealt with open heart

So many builders descend
shaking out paint dust clothes
where raspberries want to grow
Hammering, shouting, idisregard

Last night's dream so wondrous
all of us working with ease
Best we can with what we got
Bob, I, Plum Village friends

I awoke so hopeful
thinking builders' noise done
Feeling so positive
about transformation at base

So inspired by Thay's recovery
just breathing and smiling
practicing physiotherapy
Accepting life as is

*   *   *

Sun through bird's free flight
Touching Mom's serenity
on solid Earth nature walk
After neighbour uncooperative

It's the last straw to shift
into wide dimension vision
He has actions' consequences
of causing such suffering

And I felt so released
from mind arguing tangles
knowing I'd done what I could
to try to normalise relations

I'd started by saying hello
though he hadn't even told us
there'd be this much more noise
while it impacts upon us

So I'm satisfied with my actions
though I couldn't manage a smile
Now in wonder of Light 'n Beauty
sporadic drilling sounds come through

*   *   *

Bulbs' inspiration
Peaking leaf heads out
as I clear dried cement drips
and chips of brickwork

Strawberries overgrow them
Hard earth stomped by builders
None of these stop bulb sprouts
from reappearing once again

Indomitable spirit
of life force continuation
Reusing, transforming
I gain energy from you

Taking time to recuperate
from difficult five months
of intense noise, disruption
Neighbours' unskilful actions

Coming back to True Self
Watching, understanding
Exposing deep hurt
to splendour of nature

Compassionate detachment
from relational connection
to neighbours, thought were friends
Cutting cord for healing space

20 January 2015

***Wrote this for my dear Reiki student
who suddenly passed away***

Dear Sheila Barlow
Reiki Master Teacher
Student and friend
A part of Reiki energy

You continue in that flow
in so many ways
Through all those you touched
loved and cared for

Feeling your presence
Giving Reiki after your death
and at our Reiki group share
Yes, do join us at them all

Remembering your story
of doing Reiki on clients
you cared for in sheltered
housing
and how much it helped them

Their parents thanked you
One woman who couldn't speak
would came over, take your
hands
and put them on her for
treatment

Learning Reiki enthusiastically
to the highest level
Practicing regularly on yourself
meditating, growing so much

Your wide laugh and sharing
will be sorely missed
Sending Reiki and a smile
to your essence Dear Sheila

22 January – 8 February 2015

Other side neighbours move
It's the end of a sweet era
Saying farewell to Mariam
Blessing the house with her

Remember, she says
how you came in the night
to help me with my labour
right here in the hallway

I tell her and Hamilton
felt energy connection
Been through so much together
including their births

Their home where their family
grew from one child to four
Was so right to give Reiki
and support when I could

She said feeling stronger
with more space they needed
She gives me her candle
We hug once again

I speak of love re-blooming
Yes, here for new neighbours
and our continued friendship
I'll cycle out to see her

*   *   *

New neighbours moving in
We all want to get on
Made sure they were included
Got to know them at local party

Accepting that they'll
build car park on front garden
Certainly their right
which I'll have to get used to

And what I must accept
with party wall neighbours
is not able to make it right
though we've made many efforts

A monk once told me
after person was unreasonable
'Some people are like that'
I see resolution is letting go

*   *   *

New other side neighbours
chainsaw down all their trees
Bringing in needed light
But sadness at destruction

He says just beginning
They'll plant new bushes
I agree to cut on our side
right by adjoining fence

Yes, all transformations
and they told us beforehand
Now wider vista to river
But I do still feel shaken

Sanding noise through party wall
Sunday during Reiki attunements
Told students nothing to do with us
just before we started ritual

Energy still focused, deep
as I let go further of control
Seeing my need to be right
and how it's an obstruction

157

Explaining to Manas
with kind awareness
that won't exist at all
if worry, fear ends body

'We have to take care of her'
I started hearing recently
Combined aspects of Joy
bringing forth realisation

So healthy for me
to come into this place
Though gelling takes endurance
Sturdy, solid on the earth

*   *   *

Find The Worst, Manas
separate or as one
brings worry, sleepless night
Hurting my body

If too fearful that my actions
will be harmful to others
Brings harm to this person
it's not helpful to anyone

In untangling to clarity
can see/feel compassion
rising for this being
who so wants to do right

Somewhere deep within
still afraid that seen as 'bad'
will bring unloving separation
when I so want to be embraced

Knowing family did love me
even if at times scapegoated
I can transform with understanding
bringing more lucid perceptions

Severing habit link
developed in six months
between loudness and headache
making me sound sensitive

Coming back to true home
wonder of Bob's bond
'Our love will see us through'
as he told me with a cuddle

Him painting in studio
Me enjoying conservatory
To any noise next door
relaxing, saying, 'safe within'

That instinctive bracing
that's come in my body
to who knows what noise is next
I shall smile to with love

*   *   *

Studio complete
Outer painting finished
Second coat so yellow
shines in bright sunshine

Bob reworking his painting
not really spoiled after all
Big Rock Candy Mountain
continued on Fannie's birthday

Both of us make reconnections
with family back in the States
Each doing it in our own way
Me planning visit for wedding

16 February 2015

Kerin's moving to London
She managed on her own
to work out the exchange
So it's going to happen

Lots of varied details
for us to help with
Now wishing her well
Hoping for the best

Letting go of feeling
this isn't adventageous
She'll have less support from us
and may see daughter less

But after so many years
of her trying to move
and disliking Cambridge
she's made up her mind

So what can I do
but just let it flow
Seems a good flat in Fulham
Kevin checked it out with her

I'll be here for Sophie
and so will Bob
We'll help settle Kerin
into new London life

Hope that she's able
to make fresh start she wants
I love you and send Reiki
Let it go, let it flow

17 February 2015

Cousin Emily visits
on undergrad exchange
Meeting new generation
of childhood cousin Harry

Raising her with meditation
in City Yoga tradition
Parents surround her with love
creative arts, bioscience

Now far from home
thoughtful, exploring
We meditate together
I give her Cambridge tour

Us speaking to Helen
Harry heard in background
Now with speech difficulties
We connect beyond space, time

I show Emily photos
of her great-great-grandparents
Tell how great-grandma's suffragist
Speak of many family lives

I know this pleases Dad
who so identified with Harry
Emily's kind talk with Kerin
Now she's off to meet Kev, Ella

Such warmth, love and sorrow
Heart touched in many ways
Emily happy with family links
So good she could join us

19 February 2015

22 February 2015

At Phouc and Phung's
Year of Sheep warmth
Our ancestors, cultures
unite in Oneness beauty

Meeting up for Ella's birthday
Joy of healthy granddaughters
growing thoughtfully, creative
The beauty of our family

With Sangha at Tet
New Years Eve opening
for ancestors to join us
Spiritual, biological

Ella's celebration
She's so very excited
with Sophie, best friends
They go off and play

Feeling their power
as we sit together
Watching, I find within
how I give myself hard time

Loved-one stressed out
about her move to London
But she had a good city trip
positive with family, friends

Another deeper layer
coming up to be released
Asking ancestors' support
to transform to freedom

I'll put aside time
to help her after move
Before going to the States
want to settle her with a cat

Seeing how destructive
to this person and others
Distraction supports staying
at level of injured me

Being here for Sophie
reconnection on Friday
Relieved her virus past
Getting on well in school

In ceremony I read
how time of forgiveness
Starting with myself
my undermining worry

Her resilience, solidity
such a blessing to us all
Glad she'll still share with me
thoughts, experiences, projects

Forgiveness spreading out
to unskilful neighbours
Not wanting to hold on
to this anger, resentment

So much her own person
with her own views
That's also important
vision as she grows up

Building sense of safety
So I can feel more at home
in myself and my house
Understanding, letting go

28 February 2015

3 March 2015

Turning Sixty-Eight
Year Bob and I met
Family soon gathering
to celebrate my birthday

Being in family love
flowing through me
Resonating out, back

Intertwined in happiness
Gifts of togetherness
Reflecting warmly on

Through joys, difficulties
we grow and transform
Supporting, enriching

Like bird's wings in flight
momentum continues
Gliding with safe currents

Changing with the flow
yet essentially connected
Being in family love

Being 68 with Bob
sharing this day together
Grateful for such blessings
Aware of fear of death

Better to observe it
than hide under activity
Wanting to do gardening
but first embracing scared

I understand what Thay meant
about how we don't die
and on some levels feel that
Yet birthday brings up hollow

Good, I noticed
so I can hold you kindly
Won't always be here like this
making this a sacred day

Bob says will be good year
that our love will see us through
Clearly base for that is Now
savouring sweetness together

He gives me his painting
of Salema beach in colour
Supporting, affirming practice
of receiving pink acceptance

So much on
So need to stop
Buildup growing
toward Kerin's move

Momentum strong
Form filling for her
rubbish pick ups
repacking, de-hoarding

Neighbour noise restarts
building barriers again
I wrestle back focus
to my inner stability

Singing to Avalokita
Compassion for me
As I near US trip
Need to be in good space

Asking Reiki to heal
through this whole phase
for me, Bob, Kerin
May her fresh start go well

*   *   *

Flower fresh mindfulness
blossoms in teaching
for Reiki students and I
as we cross-pollinate

Practicing together
various meditations
our stems intertwine
Supporting each other

Thay's stream waters plant
Reiki energy flows through
Usui Mikao smiles
Continuing his intension

Kerin's move is part
of how things change
Cycles flowing through
strength of our love

Sophie, Bob's voices
drift up as I type
Pancakes, he's making her
as many times before

She asks for our key
and we give it to her
A continuation gesture
We'll still be here for you

Bob calls it a celebration
Korma dinner tonight
For years Kerin said would move
Now it's finally happening

*   *   *

Flower revenge
Planting bulbs
by neighbours' brick wall
Reversing the energy

As Tai Chi non-resistance
Stable Dantian on Earth
So safe from incursions
Grounded with gravity

Converting trampled soil
to bed of bright blossoms
that we can watch sprout
Though building noise again

Unpredictability
makes it more difficult
But prompts to stay present
in mindfulness of flow

17 March 2015

Last week so hard
helping Kerin pack
then yesterday the move
which went OK in the end

Still details to work out
but need to let go
No pressure as before
We all need healing time

Bob took Cat to London
and today is exhausted
I managed to ground head spin
Feet solid on earth

In previous days
discovering such panic
fear and resentment
Embracing them all

So relieved now move's over
wasn't sure stuff would fit in van
or that we could get it packed
But thankfully that's passed

Family action together
Kev helped in London too
I finished off in old flat
took last meter reading

Just did best I could
would've liked to clean more
But broom was also moved
apologised, left readings

Wanted to be perfect
never getting upset at Cat
Then I wouldn't be human
to build compassion for me, others

21 March 2015

Releasing to relief
after day helping Kerin
Planned pick up of new cat
falls apart in morning

Keep trying to make it happen
for fear of her disappointment
Then when I get to her place
see still so much to unpack

Working throughout day
organising, disposing
It becomes clear
it's too early for a cat

Yes, she's disappointed
and not happy with me
But it passes over time
with stable efforts to help her

Working to let go
of what I think is best
How would I know anyway
Just flow positive with conditions

By evening I've managed
to get living room together
Cat happy, appreciative
Catharsis for us both

Hanging up Buddha plaque
found in an odd box
brought feeling as I left
that it shined through the flat

Kerin wanting to learn
how to travel to Cambridge
to come back to see Sophie
While she's ready for new start

22 – 25 March 2015

27 March 2015

Stability from here, now
to view my perceptions
and how I look upon them
as Mom used to say

At time of her birthday
I know she is with me
supporting my efforts
to practice with Nature

Kerin calling last night
on phone with her too long
Getting off at near eleven
Need Compassionate Detachment

She doesn't have help in London
This has made it harder
Hopefully things will settle
Nurturing positive not fear

*   *   *

Yesterday in tears
Bob holds my hand
says it's good to cry
stroking my shoulder

So lucky to be with him
healthy, in house together
Kids finding own ways
Granddaughters as well

Being kind enough to accept
worry when it arises
Embracing me with love
Seeing I don't know what's best

Shifting focus to US trip
after windows put in
Cat settling in own way
Bob, Kev will support her

Time to let go and pack
Enjoying light in bedroom
that new window provides
Clean and simple release

It's good to have a space
away from so much stress
Hopefully perspective
family warmth, reunion

I know sister has own ways
and I need to stay aware
But I do so want to see her
And could use a change

So many years apart
though I call her on phone
She doesn't ever call me
but I accept that, not tangled

May I have the mindfulness
central equilibrium
to enjoy being with sister
with Compassionate Detachment

Challenges ahead
travel, room arrangements
May Reiki flow with us
and be here with family

10- 13 April 2015

Jetlagged jumble
but in a nice way
Body, mind landing
in it's own time

After good visit
with sister, free from cancer
Wedding worked out well
Newark, Brooklyn reacquainted

Flying back home
to Bobbie's love
Reassembling my life
with fresh insights

Allowing new era
to begin from here
Letting go
of old worry, fears

Building faith
with original family
Strengthening our love
Seeing all have difficulties

*   *   *

Beauty of family
shining such love
for me and each other
So glad I went

Reconnection
to ancient roots
still alive in earth
of childhood soil

My sister loves me
Transforming 'bad'
family misperception
Role further reversed

Strength of bond legacy
of dear Mom and Dad
Positive ways of seeing
and being with us

Opening my heart
Clearing my mind
Meditating with Susan
and sweet cousin Eddie

Seeing niece, sharing wedding
with nephew, great nieces
They hope to connect
with granddaughters here

*   *   *

Cousin Eddie
eyes wide to enjoy
Seeing the best
in this moment

He who taught me
'Good I noticed'
His mom said smile
to be beautiful

Ruty and Mom
strong sister link
We their children
having our own

Love waves through
genes intertwined
Childhood memories
Life being now

Physical distance
but when together
though it's so rare
Connection clear, warm

165

18 - 22 April 2015

KERIN GETS A CAT

Cat meets new cat
in day out together
through London on tubes
with big, empty cat box

Then bus to Battersea
Dog and Cat Shelter
Us so hoping they will
have one to take home

Forms and interviews
waiting to find out
We watch Charlie beckon
Will a balcony be enough

Cat says this one's like her
looking for safe, stable home
After having a rocky time
he's looking for affection

Though earlier anaesthetic
Charlie, Cat introduced
After initial sniff
Charlie warms to touch

He purrs as Cat pets
and strokes his head
Charlie rolls onto her hand
Yes, he wants more

Cat now in tears
runs fingers through fur
They bond with solidity
Even touch heads

They can help each other
heal and make new life
One cat, one person
to support one another

But can't take Charlie home
as vet needs to check him
So dear Bob goes in today
to London for Cat's birthday

Her present's picking up cat
even though Bob's allergic
After birthday lunch together
Cat'll complete her move

Moving's so stressful
though pressured, did well
Now can truly settle in
Cat getting new cat

*   *   *

Sophie, Cat birthday party
Being back with the girls
Kerin takes tube, train here
First time on her own

Kevin finishes CD
of Mindfulness For Reiki
Joint project coalesces
as conditions are right

26 April 2015

Kev got PhD funding
Celebrating together
with Ella, Bob, Helena
Happy dancing, shouting

Wondrous and shocking
after all these years of trying
His persistence and insights
pay off in the end

Leaving FE's life changing
after 14 years of teaching
To research full time
What a special gift

Helena makes us lunch
Joyfully we toast Kevin
Hard work and kindness
such a winning combination

Wearing Mom, Fannie's jewellery
knowing ancestors *kvell* too
Such warm-hearted rosiness
Family blessings to share

Savouring this moment
New era unfolding
all so proud and pleased
Kev got PhD funding

27 April 2015

Cat's London fresh start
settled in with new cat
Writing about her pet
for book project with Bob

We all go out for treats
Both offspring doing well
Celebrating Kev's news too
with Bob, Helena, Ella

Cat's moved to a nice area
allowing her baggage release
Transforming past difficulties
in gradual life-change process

Naturally there's ups and downs
Breathing stability underpinning
I send her trust, good wishes
as does loving family

Appreciating her writing
and her capabilities
Together at her local café
Cat's London fresh start

29 April 2015

Back to Nirvana
Accepting happiness
No need for perfection
just returning to beauty

That's what ancestors want
What this life is for
Why I was named *Simcha*
'Ve just vant you should be happy'

And that's the transformation
for all generations
Their torments leading to
abundant *Naches*

Understanding's the way
Composting rotting weeds
in this garden of energy
So spring blooms anew

All these misperceptions
Need for achievement
Responsaholic guilt
based in such fear

May Reiki flow to sources
Healing, Oh, so deeply
May I love myself enough
to open to my Compassion

Compassion for angst
of 'bad' misperception
Feeding panic drive
unhelpful, unnecessary

Awareness watching mind spin
through such long-term ruts
Staying solid on Mother Earth
Seeing, smiling, uncaught

Into this very moment
of such special grace
I just want to savour
Grateful for blessings

Family doing well
Each on own path
No need to fear Evil Eye
will jinks if I write this

Building blocks to future
from positivity now
Also unknown conditions
but this is what I can do

Accepting myself enough
to understand and hug
Leaving judgement behind
Coming Back to Nirvana

1 – 5 May 2015

ARRIVED AT ORDER OF INTERBEING RETREAT

A good dose of Yin
that's what we need
Solid and steady
quiet and slow

Amazed at how much
has been going on
Caught in whirlwind
working my way through

Boiler broke down
calling and packing
Just time to backup
computer before I left

Builds and moves
travels and teaching
planning and writing
Such a good time to Stop

*   *   *

See Nirvana in everything
Sister Annabel tells us
Stepping beside her
happiness, bluebells spread

Though can see Nirvana
in beauty of outstretched tree
Nagging worries within
Fear trusting Store Consciousness

She says let Mind Consciousness
garden the seeds so well
But also let innate insights
in Store ripen, rise up

What about unwholesome seeds
Maybe will bring false positives
rather than true wisdom
Could they misguide me

But practice helps Mind
nurture good seeds in Store
Concentration of fertiliser
supports clarity to grow strong

Now sheep begin to bah
'Don't take it so seriously'
In healing relief
releasing back to Nirvana

*   *   *

My birthless nature
revealing itself
in smell remembered as child
Consciousness before person

This consciousness evolving
continuing, flowing
way past this body
Here before its formation

My dearest Bob
seeing you beyond body
Orchestras before birth
playing in boyhood head

My intimate life partner
I depend on you so much
for advice (sometimes rejected)
Your love and support

Very dearest Bobbie
I know our bodies will cease
But our energies so interflow
that we'll continue together

6 May 2015

Net of Indra, 3-D
Each jewel connected
to interwoven strands

Light shining out from one
reflects on all jewels
All reflecting on One

Interconnection beauty
so easy when release
ruts of misperceptions

Old 'bad' film still running
I reach out, touch the screen
Now knowing what it is

And I am learning truth
that seeds are just potentials
so Store's perfect, amoral

It's only when seeds manifest
in my Mind Consciousness
that they take on moral value

But Mind can embrace
unwholesome seeds with wisdom
of Mindfulness Trainings

Not having to fear innate 'bad'
such spaciousness opens
Expensiveness of bright energy

It naturally reflects
Bodhisattvas in all directions
Net of Indra, 3-D

7 May 2015

Completing time on TOIC
Being on The OI Council
for agreed three year stint
after group that formed it

So many details
and teleconferences
emails and emotional
ups and downs

Working together
to act in mindful way
Often achieving this
though old habits stalk

Learning from the experience
Creating helpful projects
like Fee Reduction Support
to help OIs afford retreats

Proposing the basis
of our training retreats
like last wondrous one
All with Sister Annabel

Her awareness and wisdom
helping us learn together
Retreats being long enough
for insights to jell

So glad TOIC'll continue
that I found two new members
and clarified disharmony
at our last meeting

My head still spins
as I slowly let go
Trusting energy beyond me
Completing time on TOIC

SHOCK TORY WIN

Digesting Tory win
Shocking, unexpected
Poor Britain, Europe
trapped in austerity mindset

Processing the grief
of Tory election win
Suffering of vulnerable
as cutbacks continue

As I look deeper
I find we're all affected
Compassion for myself
Compassion for Britain

We'll work in lots of ways
toward progressive change
But clearly UKIP vote
was based in profound fear

Fear of those different
'other' in many contexts
From Manas, 'me' protection
misperceptions follow easy

So very important part
of bringing just harmony
is using Reiki, Mindfulness
to transform reactive fear

Fear can also be unlearnt
as we gain more perspective
Seeing interconnections
we need for our survival

Intermeshed Indra Net
such jewels shining out
Reflecting, as I let go
of blinkers to see it

This is my true work
Bodhisattva vow
to transform myself
Help others do the same

It's what I can do
in five year Tory reign
Rooted in Earth's nurture
Releasing the limits

*   *   *

Water reflecting light
upon outstretched branch
Tree reflected through
gentle passing ripples

Ducks on the bank
Father feeds bread
to son in pushchair
Then to the quackers

Accepting all passers by
speaking various languages
From different races
we are all one people

Seeing Nirvana in everything
Everything in Nirvana
The whole so much more
than the sum of life's parts

18 – 19 May 2015

In ease of gentle rain
it's so very pleasant
Peace of magic house
where I attuned sisters

A miracle to pass Reiki
to women eager, open
to align for own healing
Shared experience together

Coming to appreciate
more time in Nirvana
Accepting such blessings
to hold you, my dear fear

You, too, can relax
in this mindful energy
guarding without tightness
Awareness watching over us

All aspects of this person
please come under umbrella
Don't have to shiver in cold rain
when it's cosy with safe embrace

Releasing the unknown
No need to keep spinning
possible dreaded scenarios
which aren't really happening

Better in now beauty
to be happy this instant
Savouring vivid sweetness
Best building blocks for future

Dream of tightrope walking
Keeping eyes ahead
Knowing I won't fall
if I stay focused

Stepping above play park
even flying low
Just with awareness
of body in nature

Being at home
with birdsong and river
Heron appears
watching sparkling waters

Rain drops begin
nurturing growth
Sprouting greenness
plants stretch wide

And I do the same
without even trying
Just enjoying the quiet
Savouring Heaven

20 May 2015

READ THIS AT PHUNG'S RETIREMENT PARTY

Thank you dear Phung
For your treatments and wisdom
Needle placement and advice

Thank you dear Phung
for being my friend
Hugs and laughter

Thank you dear Phung
for speaking with my daughter
on your days off when she needed it

Thank you dear Phung
for opening your heart
and house to the Sangha

Thank you dear Phung
for years of meditation
in your living room Temple

Thank you dear Phung
for your love and healing
Helping so many people

Thank you dear Phung
for sharing Vietnamese culture
food, Buddhist insights

Thank you dear Phung
for being an example
for transforming difficulties

Thank you dear Phung
for your skill and judgement
as an expert acupuncturist

Thank you dear Phung
for doing things your own way
The way you feel is right

Thank you dear Phung
for being who you are
a True Bodhisattva

For fearful windy whirls
Knowing best I can do
is allow me to be at ease
Just let it all go

Kevin's funding tangles
Kerin's uncertainties
Bob's Tory concerns
Me finishing up projects

Sadness of austerity
Mean contractions, greed
Not getting caught in worry
but building stable kindness

Yes, signing petitions
and still go on Demos
But more than that's needed
for true change to happen

*   *   *

Seeing the worry dreams
varied and vivid
Recognising what they are
At least when I'm awake

Though different content
the theme is the same
Not tragic or nightmares
but unsettling spin

Seeds arising
Fearful problems to solve
Keep trying this or that
for me and other people

Unresolved troubles
organising that's not real
Bursting forth to surface
Keeping me busy, anxious

Waking feeling shaken
Then slow realisation
that my life's good when
not caught in these tangles

*   *   *

Healing Find The Worst
waking me in the night
Niggling back to consciousness
that I'd done something wrong

Then discovering I didn't
but old trick replayed
Sending kindness to Manas
wanting to stay in control

Reikiing this morning
for transformation to sources
to release and enjoy family
Realising fear of Evil Eye

Old Jewish habit
to bless in reverse
if seen to be too happy
Oh, my God, what'll happen!

Watching, accepting
Sitting with, holding heart
In warmth of supporting pump
so much more encompassed

Kev, Helena call from Amsterdam
Ella slept well, was drawing
All doing fine, having fun
Bob laughing with Ella

So worry is unnecessary
but still feel am pushing
Wanting it to all go well
when best thing's to relax

CULMINATIONS

Finished CDs arrive
I Reiki them all
May people be helped
by this Culmination

Relaxing in Nirvana
of CD come together
After a year of energies
from Thay, Kev and I

Now full Earth cycle
since Plum Village Retreat
Thay's inspiring dharma talk
planting Mindfulness project seeds

Then moulding in my own way
CD content and course
Based on Thay's teachings
Usui Sensi's Reiki

Exploration, learning
Kabit-Zin's stress reduction
Into mix of my experience
born as fresh creation

So pleased to see it manifest
with Kev's iconic graphics
Our time together rerecording
till conditions were right

Now here in physical form
May it help many people
connect with Mindfulness, Reiki
Stress Reduction, Transformation

*   *   *

Flowing through this half term
Enjoying with Sophie, Ella
Wondrous mix in their own ways
of Mom, Dad, Fannie, Ed

Kevin's great news
born from his efforts
Given enough funds
to finish his PhD

*   *   *

Listening to my CD
at night when couldn't sleep
Deep Relax combination
perfect words, energy for me

From new perspective
able to send more kindness
to bowel I've been holding
without realising was grasping

*   *   *

Mal reads her poem with zest
of how fossils are formed
The old rocks take it all in
surrounding her on her stall

Church bells chime background
Fitting for her story
of glaziers and oceans
which help to make her friends

Their tangible evidence
of creatures long gone
collapse time to knowing
that life itself is short

But then again it evolves
into new appearances
Like the amazing fossil
she shows me with wonder

Post your poem on your stall
I encourage her with glee
Since she took all her cash
and invested in more fossils

22 – 26 June 2015

LOVE PEOPLE, NOT MONEY

Marching with whole family
for peace and justice
Grandkids made the signs
So special together

Fannie, Ed are smiling
There with us so strong
All pleased Kerin's improving
May it continue

Kevin tells of PhD
now, happily, fully funded
And redundancy payment
taking pressure off to study

Sophie's so big now
Almost as tall as me
Starting to look teenaged
Her and Ella still so bonded

A quarter of a million
people demonstrate to say
Austerity is not the way
to fairness and harmony

Sophie's poster I carry
sums it up so well
'Love People Not Money'
May it ripple out

*   *   *

Generosity of Spirit
stretching wide-open
to boatpeople in Med
frightened and desperate
Some dieing along the way

Generosity of Spirit
sending migrants Reiki
and those with misperceptions
seeing them as a threat
Loosing their own humanity

Generosity of Spirit
reaching back to grandparents
in Steerage on boats themselves
Hoping for good conditions
and support to start fresh

Generosity of Spirit
starting fresh each breath
Savouring the air
through lungs down to belly
Grounded with Earth's Nurturing

*   *   *

Bodhicitta roses blooming
Red, broad, smiling
From Sangha gift plant
and in my heart

In world with bloody wars
starving, hurt people
May compassion ease burdens
held in Collective Store

1-2 July 2015

FEMALE SPIRITUAL ANCESTORS

Caroline Rhys Davids
Inspiring English Buddhist
Though women's subjugation
she was not caught in it

One of the first women
to receive BA, Masters
She lectured in Buddhist history
and published prolifically

Advocate for social justice
Women's suffrage
Children's rights
Compassion for poor

Beyond action she practiced
living, being the Dharma
Using knowledge and insight
to translate Pali texts

In harmony with husband
Son dies in World War I
Beyond tragedy, renewal
Growing, deepening understanding

With clarity of mind
seeing into Buddhist past
Through vehicle of Pali
and her spiritual practice

Reinterpreting the Dharma
Bring light to women's role
Making Therigatha accessible
Transmitting courage to females

Buddha knew we could enlighten
and with words of nuns who did
We nurture determination
to practice with ease and smile

So many sisters run through me
with the Dharma in our veins
Together mind, hearts open
with Caroline Rhys Davids

*   *   *

Female spiritual ancestors
rising up within me
Goddess Priestesses for Peace
whose names are long lost
Your nurturing still resonates

Buddhist Sisters of Therigatha
Nuns attaining enlightenment
Mahapajapati and disciples
Patacara, teachers, mothers
wise women, wanders, Crones

Miriam, guarding sister of baby Moses
Arranging mother's care at Pharaoh's
Leading dance, song after Red Sea crossing
Spiritual leader, source of nurture, healing
Miriam's Well providing water in desert

Harriet 'Moses' Tubman
Felt heaven reaching freedom
Returned to free a thousand slaves
Using insight, survival with nature
dreams, visions, charisma, faith

I touch the Earth in connection
with gratitude for inspiration
Your energy comes through to me
to continue in new/old ways
Female spiritual ancestors

I will be sick in bed
sometime in the future
wishing for today's blessings
So I'll appreciate them now

During wakeful night
I listen to Deep Relax
Softening, releasing
What a great relief

Appreciating hands and feet
allowing me to do so much
Heart and digestive organs
keeping this person alive

So many blessing
I gratefully accept
When not taken for granted
surely enough for happiness

There are also challenges
How else would I understand
grow, nurture compassion
Ways of seeing such beauty

Connecting with the Earth
Up from depths I hear
From immeasurable time
you have been free

*   *   *

Slipping back into Nirvana
Remembering the way
of ease and open brain
Sinking solid into Earth

Seeing how I fall out
into rut of default despair
Waking to it some mornings
Worry spinning during day

So good to notice
That's best to do
Then just let go
as Thay's hand motion

Just keep letting go
is what he advised
Yes, I feel release
flowing through body

*   *   *

Grounded not Grasping
Well, moving between them
Releasing best I can
with my back out and sore

Grounded not grasping
House issues to deal with
Conservatory leaks
Fence guy hasn't come

Grounded not grasping
Allowing Zonar to soften
that place where pain holds
Gradually reducing

Grounded not grasping
as traveller sings, chats
Taught him Reiki 1
many years before

Grounding not grasping
end of teaching term
Yesterday two pregnant women
So wondrous to share Reiki

Grounding not grasping
Bob's gone to get his brother
So good for them to be together
Barry's laughter'll burst forth

13 –22 July 2015

COMPASSIONATE RIPPLES

Poor children weaken all of us
Their deprivation is ours
Society pays in the long run
for this tragic human deficit

May this insight strike
George Osborne, David Cameron
Elitely educated at Eton
away from family, caring

Shrinking hearts and the State
can't bring true happiness
Reality of interdependence
shatters illusion of separation

Compassion wells up
for innocent young ones
Victims of Tory cuts
Conservative mindset

And to the parents
working so hard
to feed their kids
Worried, now what to do

Such sadness, despair
I feel, watch within
Knowing transformation's
best way to help us all

That energy ripples out
in so many ways
Petitions, demos, writing
Contributing to feeding hungry

I wish the Tories hadn't won
There wasn't extreme greed
Surprisingly that's what's happened
I need to acceptance that

*   *   *

Compassionate ripples
Drops of rain in still river
Spreading widening circles
Seeing, further and broader

In so many ways
I can't save the world
Yet nurturing compassion inward
waves naturally increase out

Sent to those who suffer
via energy vibrations
Not sapping my own
Unfolding through greater whole

So glad to hear EU family
has not broken up
Finding ways forward
after yet more negotiations

May Greek people prosper
Not have to live under yoke
of unfair debt upon them
May paymasters transform

*   *   *

We support you IMELDA sisters
Campaigning through performanc
for women's basic right
to control her own body

Generations joining forces
in the London Irish stream
of energy and beauty
love, life and art

May the tide turn toward reason
Converting fear to understanding
of women's contributions
We support you IMELDA sisters

29 July 2015

NEW GENERATION TOGETHER

Fresh generation connects
Girls come from across the sea
Together for the first time
All my parents' great grandchildren

Nephew Dan clearly touched
remembering Mom and Dad
Showing kids magic tricks
originating from my father

Cousins quickly bond
Similarities clear
and differences too
Each growing in own way

From original seeds
stretching back so far
before my parents and theirs
All generations *kvell*

Though ancestors never met
these beautiful, sweet girls
I am their witness
seeing future before us

Youngsters sprouting well
Each as own person
to go forth with our love
and our family energy

Talking with Dan
Watching him with Kev
speaking with Kerin
All hugging and sharing

Photographing it all
to send to my sister
Now we're top age group
entrusting new generations

I'm often shocked
Coming into living room
finding my granddaughters
there so big, grown

Sophie as tall as me
Ella up to collarbone
Their closeness heart-opening
Playing, common interests

Such wondrous momentum
preparing for family retreat
Misgivings and hope
Smiling, feeding positive

May the retreat go well
Helpful to Kerin, Sophie
May I have patience, solidity
Compassionate Detachment

*   *   *

7 -14 August 2015

Last night's sudden outburst
of anger from Bob and I
Letting energy settle
Where did it come from?

Built up pressure
we hadn't noticed
Boiled under surface
until it exploded

So startling and jolting
Neither of us wanted it
Yet somehow it happened
Propelling us to different realm

Walking on the Green
taking time to return to senses
Then starting to speak
Levelling with each other

Wanting to ask and say
what was bubbling in caldron
Coming back for tea and talk
on a deeper plane

Shaken by it all
Want to avoid this next time
We certainly didn't like this rush
Just want to return to earth

More insight of Bob's feelings
and him of mine
Further understanding
How to better communicate

*   *   *

.

After seven months of noise
such difficult disruption
I can finally let go, resolve
now that build's settled, ended

Understanding, Forgiveness
Seeing next-door trapped
in their own weaknesses
of greed, grasping, pain

I continue to say hello
Couldn't live so close and not
But limiting it to that
I hope, more often, to add a smile

Smiling to my pain
of betrayal and hurt
Nourishing healing
Releasing to new era

*   *   *

After caught in cyberspace
rejoining physical body
Enticed by new phone
so fast on the web

Seemingly much smoother
less jangly I think
So staying on it later
Paying price in the night

Returning to remember
my computer rule of thumb
No emailing after 9 pm
Better unwind toward sleep

Morning stepping by river
Rippling through to clarity
It's longing that entranced me
Coming back to reality

15 August 2015

Walkin' with my guys
down by the Ouse
Tributary of Cam
wild with flowers, reeds

By meadow along bank
we stop for our lunch
Resting in heaven
with Kevin and Bob

So peaceful and lazy
in warm summer space
to just be together
in ease of our love

Nature surrounds us
with beauty so pure
Purple, yellow flowers
she planted herself

Walking on, why not
Try the longer route
toward Hemingford Abbots
Let's just explore

Playing it by ear
seeing how we feel
Foliage on other shore
with vast shades of green

Speaking to strangers
passing us from other way
They encourage us on
We rest then continue

So great to be with Kev
His energy so fresh
Soon to start new life
doing full time PhD

Him feeling lighter
the oomph's contagious
Transported to new place
we all can let go

Not that far from Cambridge
but Busway's opened up
a route to go out freely
into deeper countryside

Pools of lakes
swans and grasslands
Flooded in winter
but welcoming now

Resting near small beach
without an agenda
We're heartened to go on
up toward the Old Mill

Past thatched cottages
Finding pub to quench thirst
I get ice cream
Savouring smooth sharing

Stepping over bridges
and into campsite
Kev remembers childhood
of us camping in the van

Back following Ouse again
on thicket path toward
St Ives, ancient river town
Amazed how far we've walked

Encouraging each other
in so many ways
Nurturing the positive
Walkin' with my guys

30 – 31 August 2015

WONDROUS FAMILY RETREAT

Miracle Mindfulness Retreat
in Stourbridge again
Where eighteen years before
Thay taught the Sangha

Back this time without
his physical body
But he's so very present
in Monastics, lay disciples

Thay's continuations
blossoming all round
in Children's Programme
Nine Teens take Five Trainings

Through sitting, lying down
walking on Mother Earth
Touching her solidity
we return to true home

Sister Natasha, Brother Ben
here in their homeland
to spread British Dharma
for us to easily digest

Vietnamese heritage
brings tender wisdom
through Thay Phap Ung
and sisters, brothers

Happiness in Dharma Sharing
Retreatants are satisfied
Not needing Thay physically
to find him in Monastics

We grow through the week
Nearly three hundred fifty
beings practicing as one
Sangha of transformation

Some are new to Mindfulness
Others there for Thay's planting
We return to Magnolia tree
Now taller than us

The veil gently opens
revealing the Ultimate
right here inside us
so interconnected

Universal cosmic light
shines in smiling faces
Through our clearer eyes
nature's beauty captivates

We reach out, embrace
sing No Coming, No Going
So many get the trainings and
The Miracle of Mindfulness

*   *   *

I am you
Thay Phap Ung says
tapping me on the shoulder
when I thank him for dharma talks

I feel it that moment
in the wonder of Oneness
Veil opened wide
to reveal Goddess Nature

Leaves waving to us
Cloud break through to
orange-pink sunset
Round in my heart

In transmission ceremony
I retake 14 Trainings
Feel smile revealed
in my pumping vessel

9 September 2015

FOR DEAR FRIEND SHEILA ROBIN

Sheila dear friend
so a part of me
Even in your passing
you live on in us

So generous, responsible
Pivotal in my life
Opening your new flat
to my family in '83

Staying a month
we had time to settle
Find a place of our own
back in the UK

It wasn't just staying
but all your advice
Offer tea to workers, guests
Shop at M&S when you can

Your caring so wide
and worries as well
Taking on the world's burdens
Working tirelessly for justice

From when we first met
in '70 in Women's Lib
to your visit a month ago
our friendship's matured

So supportive of others
Your mother, Anna, nieces
Concerned for their well being
Mellowing yourself near the end

Doing Transcendental Meditation
Letting me give you Reiki
Glimpsing nature's ease
Our wondrous Interbeing

And in that vast web
you are still so very present
Your amazing drive, energy
becomes available in new ways

We continue your work
You making sure I voted
Continuing your love
Sheila dear friend

*   *   *

Sheila energy at your funeral
Holding you in love circle
Releasing you to be so free
Wind gliding sails with ease

Your life an inspiration
of caring and commitment
With lesson I take onboard
about letting go of worry

So many connections
Ways you brought us together
So pivotal in our lives
Support networks continued

Hugging friends, hearts touch
Crying, sadness of our loss
Singing human race united
by our international ideal

Hearing from your family
of your help and example
Bringing us back together
to begin era without you

Yet I know you are present
within me and the wind
Blowing wondrous new ways
of Sheila energy transforming

10 September 2015

FOR SHEILA AND I

Releasing beyond ego
What a relief
I don't need to carry on
protecting an illusion

What I'd like to continue
into the future
is the positive aspects
of what's called 'Joy'

No need for this exact
formation of soul or spirit
Anyway made up
of all elements within/without

Thank you to ancestors
Biological and spiritual
Back to tiny animals
and dear Mother Earth

From you I've come
and back to you I'll go
Releasing fear of loosing
some precious misperception

What else can we do
but flow with life cycle
Water rising as steam
returning as rain

Nothing to defend
though lots to learn
Future isn't chosen later
but starting now with change

Opening to transformation
feeling it work in heart
Healing, restoring
life of body in Oneness

Lying on the earth
mourning friend Sheila
these realisations blossom
Helping us both

Nearing New Year
Jewish and academic
Enjoying the sunshine
after cloud and rain

Savouring the feel
of Common walk again
Kids and parents out
on last day before school

After summer of US
relatives for reconnection
Family Retreat success
there's autumn time for me

*   *   *

Opening to New Year
Freshness and hope
such blessings, happiness
Sadness in heart as well

Teaching Great Bright Light
to Reiki Students yesterday
Reigniting, re-inspiring
Just what I needed

So mixed the day before
Elation of new era
Jeremy Corbin elected
Huge London Refugee March

We went as a family
Sophie, Kerin, Ella
Bob, Kevin, me
All refugee descendants

*   *   *

Healing inner refugee
Opening safe space
so doesn't have to flee

Healing inner refugee
beyond outer incursions
to having place to be free

Healing inner refugee
Yellow heart smile
into coral sphere repair

Nurturing inner refugee
by noticing appearance
Accepting depth of angst

Nurturing inner refugee
in order to be clear to help
family, confused Loved-one

Loving kindness energy
softening into waves
Spiritual life force abounds

Supporting refugees worldwide
from this place of wholeness
Humanity naturally ripples out

SALEMA POEMS

Swimming in cloud
of sea/sky unbounded
Oneness of great water
Earth's gift to us

So freeing to return
to life giving essence
Releasing my burdens
of year of challenges

Sustained through practice
Bob and my love
Family bonds support
transformations to new era

Suddenly arriving
through all our steady work
Hope blossoms in collective
consciousness of caring

*   *   *

Letting go, letting go
at end of first week
Bamboo leaves wave
reminding to be happy

Into valley of Figera
descending again
Past farmed red earth
Opening to the sea

River flows out
once more home
Waves break to whiteness
Bob and I enjoy

*   *   *

Kid returns
jumping over waves
Reminiscent energy
naturally vibrates

Beyond explanation
My love for the sea
Essence within/without
together as One

*   *   *

Held in water wellness
Awareness surround
Swimming through waves
Steady, mindful strokes

Held in the ocean
wind, sand and cliffs
Recharging to continue
freshness effects

*   *   *

In sea with Ella, Kevin
Immersed in pleasure
Ella says a part of nature
I tell her Fannie said that

Jumping, riding waves
Laughing as children all
Family ocean healing
Smiling to Bob at shore

Special time together
Savouring fresh food delights
Needed break, reunion
in Salema with Kev, Ella

29 October 2015

Whole family reunited
All stay in our house
In deep connection
love, laughter, talks

Girls' half term fun
Climbing trees higher
Harry Potter pretending
Sharing special secrets

Kerin even stays over
More stable, balanced
Found church to support her
May that go well

Bob back to painting
beauty from Salema
Long chats with Kevin
them cooking in sync

Kev's exploration
of PhD expanse
Space to discover
beyond teaching pressure

Feeling wide-hearted
Grateful for three days
Love nurturing us all
in familiar resonation

Supporting creativity
each in our own ways
May muse flow happily
with family reunited

31 October 2015

Heron close up
Didn't think she'd let me
But I just come upon
her watching the waters

Such focus, concentration
as silver-blue feathers dry
Short ones stand up on head
Blowing gently in the breeze

Heron moment
Broken by rowers
Cyclist shouts orders
and she flies to other shore

*   *   *

Life close up
Didn't think I'd let me
But it just becomes vivid
watching nature's beauty

Ease of focus, concentration
when I'm really there
Thinking gone in head
Clarity flows in breeze

Only now moment
broken by worry
Manas shouts orders
I smile, return to other shore

2 November 2015

Sun streaks through
woodland space
Shining upon us
in wondrous autumn

Cycling into fog
Bob, I along river
out to Bates Bite Lock
Milton Country Park

Glimpses of red berries
Yellow leaves flourish
Water stretching through
to heart-touching beauty

Pedalling, energising
as we go along
Revitalising life
back in Cambridge

Though very different
reminiscent of cliff walks
Us together enjoying
nature in coolness

Then on arrival
sun breaks out
Warmth, such light
blessing my body

Swans glide on lake
with tall tree surround
Feeling the magic of
sun streaks through

5 – 9 November 2015

Calm beauty of Green
Not needing ocean drama
Just river gently rippling
as rain softly falls

Ripe raspberry taste
after garden regrown
from builders, disruption
Returning to peace

Resting in Nirvana
without any cares
They're just mind-objects
of which there's no need

*   *   *

Enjoying lazy day off
after Reiki teaching
Three treatments last week
All wondrous, so grateful

Miracle gift
I wanted from way back
Old calling realised
to help with love energy

Teaching, exchanging
experience with students
Mindfulness woven in
So a part of Reiki

Settled back home
delicious but tiring
Supported by sea healing
Making photo collage

Looking at pictures
I took of the water
to keep up the energy
of ocean within

14 November 2015

After Paris attack
Calling to Love
to transform fear
sadness, panic, trauma

Walking on Green
reconnecting to Earth
Solidity for balance
toward clarity of mind

In meditative focus
sending Reiki to
all those involved
for Energy of Peace

Quiet after storm
needing time to clear
beyond terror reaction
Revenge solves nothing

So what is the path
through to true safety
Surely Iraq war showed
Mid-East gets destabilised

More war adds more fuel
to anger, violence, fear
Only bringing peace home
can help it spread outward

Understanding, sharing
caring for all peoples
We move past spreading hate
into love's true protection

Beyond suffering with world
May Reiki be healing balm
Mindful energy of compassion
After Paris attack

Woman left hanging
by fingertips is me
Dream up from Store
Feels right interpretation

When I save, protect
take in and embrace
Neglected part's held
in kind, open heart

Student explains
refugee heritage
of preparing for worst
Which I see within

Surely suffered enough
as my client said
Not feeding vicious circle
She wants loving attention

Yes, I can do it
this person called Joy
Made of non-Joy elements
seeking wholeness

Allowing wholeness
Loosening 'shoulds'
Widening awareness
right through to brain

Unclenching Hara
Soften this much
Wounds transform
Being Reiki

16 November 2015

Kevin's birthday party
Nourishing our hearts
Him studying, writing
Oh, such a *mensh*

With his loving family
feeding affection
Supporting ancestors'
naches and ours

So happy for him
Having space to research
Spend time with daughter
Seeing Ella bloom

His life links with Helena
Irish-Jewish connections
Our sharing of values
deep understandings

London's past generations
Though family not there
still cultural witness
to beliefs and actions

All march now for sharing
beyond cuts and exclusion
Touching migrants in ourselves
This generation and before

With backdrop of sadness
for victims of violence
Building inner peace to shine
outward with loving family

19 November 2015

Finding myself in Nirvana
Winter garden flowers bloom
Pink and yellow so vivid
in wonder of daylight morn

With earlier afternoon darkness
appreciating the reappearance
of whiteness brightening bedroom
Awakening to joy of its arrival

Finding Nirvana in me
Sure, there's angst there too
But Nirvana is wide enough
to hold it in knowing grace

If there was only Nirvana
would I take it for granted
Poignancy of fear distraction
helps bring me back to focus

Contrasts allow such gratitude
Savouring earth's orbit of sun
In summer I miss this marvel
merely expecting longer days

Read out at twentieth
anniversary event
Presentations, food, books
as Bob turns seventy-five

Celebrating Black Apollo Press
with fellow writers and dreamers
book-lovers, life-artists
Campaigners for peace, justice

Celebrating Bob Biderman
Black Apollo Founder
Driving force behind
twenty years of vision, energy

Building on independent
publishing traditions
Innovating for new century
while writing truths from heart

Celebrating our colleagues
starting with David Kelley
bohemian, artist, Cambridge Don
Passing away in it's early years
Your energy continues with us

David Cutting, Germinal partner
Graphic designer par excellence
Retiring to pursue calling
as wondrous fine artist

Kevin Biderman, so multiskilled
Press designer, writer, artist
of sound, video, photographs
Youthful energy sees us through

All the writers that we've published
From right here in Cambridge
to France, the States, Armenia

Those alive with creative vision
and bringing back London Victorians
like Zangwill and Harkness
inspiring us to carry on

Our supporters, editors, readers
believing new models still grow
from independent publishing's
love for people, words, ideas
Not ever-expanding corporate profits

To the muse and the spirit
of a better world for us all
Allowing our caring humanity
to flower with interconnection
for collective awaking of Heart
Celebrating Black Apollo Press

*   *   *

Anniversary success
of Bob's birth and press
Event goes very well
So relieved and happy

Old friends gather round
Bob shares creative slideshow
which elucidates his vision
and the history of the press

Bob reads from new book
as do John, Olivier
The girls run bookshop
Kevin videos event

Back home for Indian meal
Ella's cake in book shape
Bob doing it his way
Anniversary success

15 December 2015

Interesting interlude
Back to Sixty-Eight
with John and Olivier
Bob and myself

All dedicated activists
in May and beyond
Coming from different angles
Intersecting at times

John leads other faction
of Student SDS
Bob and I in Jo Hill
New Left participatory

For us youth culture
also woven through
John Maoist, hierarchical
We each played our part

Later sectarian schisms
but together through Big Strike
for Ethic Studies Department
First Win at US Uni

Now four together
Olivier from Paris
where we so admired
movement for change

After spark was lit
spreading into streets
Local people discussed
new ways of seeing/being

Nearly fifty years later
we look back and share
effects on our lives
which rippled out so far

What happened to us
How other movements born
What really changed
and how the world hasn't

Some real understandings
hard to have with British friends
without similar experiences
to reminisce and examine

Yet with old comrades
other aspects very different
Them suspect of 'organised religion'
Seeing my practice as part of that

So we discuss this as well
I don't need to feel defensive
Pleased for our connections
Interesting Interlude

Out of darkness
comes the sun
Orange, pink streaks
like Bob's painting

Out of darkness
comes realisation
I've suffered enough
Intension to be happy

Out of darkness
comes the solstice
Another cycle round
Bounty to enjoy

Out of sunshine
comes the darkness
Beauty in each
season, life-phase

*   *   *

Oneness feel deepening
Sweet time with Sophie, Bob
Her coming less often now
as she grows up

Oneness feel deepening
Studying Family Tree
Bob writing of Grandma Celia
Her family killed in Holocaust

Oneness feel deepening
Reading Mom's kind, old letters
Mom saying she found serenity
hopes Kerin does in own way

Oneness feel deepening
Shifting view of my adolescence
Thinking I was so rebellious
finding thank you letter to parents

Believing, accepting
my blessings, good life
Though salt of pain lingers
now immersed in wide lake

From there I can appreciate
bulbs flowering too early
Even if snow covered later
purple violets still smile

How can I truly know
what New Year brings
Just offering positive causes
in sunshine and friendship

*   *   *

Fen returning to bog
Swans grazing on grass
Amazed at their size
when getting up close

Winter upon us
Hot ginger tea
Conservatory pleasure
Cosy light in rain

Savouring last of leftovers
Pumpkin pie from our party
Tomorrow life normalises
Grateful not to commute

Hands are so toasty
Surrounding warm cup
Cuddled up by heater
Fen returning to bog

4- 6 January 2016

Wondrous day with Kevin
My boy turned man
Thoughtful and bright
creative and loving

What a special time
to savour together
Him able to research
without teaching weight

Lightness of grant
so well deserved
Studying at British Library
freed of heavy burdens

I am so happy
to spend day with son
Talking of our projects
family, joint history

Sharing old stories
Memories galore
Travels in the van
through frozen France

Which house did you like best?
He asks over Ramen
This one for now
San Francisco for then

He liked Toulouse
Two adjoining apartments
Fun, adventure for him
Not easy time for Bob and I

Us in transition
Chaos, Kev calls it
We came through together
into Portland era

That exploration
evolved back to Britain
Happier now, I tell him
then when turning forty

So much to prove
What have I accomplished?
So relieved cured of that
into easier satisfaction

Steadily I train myself
to be more Nirvanaised
So happy Kev had a rest
with his family in Ireland

We like Calder exhibit
mobiles, shadows intrigue
Museums such a pleasure
continued through generations

*   *   *

Multicoloured bird
painted by Bob
Like stained glass window
showing through the light

It takes the contrast
to show it off well
Pleasure, some anxiety
coexist in knowing splendour

This is the way
of acceptance and beauty
Not caught in the detail
eyes can easily misperceive

And if I were the bird
my vision'd be so different
But still could enjoy
wondrous nature

Compassion for fear of fear
a source of deep dread
Bringing inertia
Why go on, do anything?

Yet such beauty, love
brings wonder energy
I want to understand
obstacle of this person

Back to *Shtetl* and before
'Chosen people' for oppression
What'll they do to us next?
Don't let Evil Eye hear blessings

So wanting to be loved
Scared I won't really be
The 'badness' 'll ruin everything
even if it's just potential

Insight, transformation
of hindrances of happiness
To be more fully free
Compassion for fear of fear

*   *   *

After numerous attempts
to find jacket in sales
Not easy for averse shopper
but finally managed it

Warm new jacket happiness
walking out on Green
Temperatures have dropped
but snug inside Raspberry

Meeting older women
also able to venture forth
We're bundled up cosy
enjoying river and foul

Light coming through
whiteness of sky
So invigorating
moving at faster pace

Still savouring footsteps
So glad to be alive
to witness seagulls soar
Swans glide on muddy water

Beyond phantom of fears
releasing so much deeper
to vivid splendour Now
Warm new jacket happiness

*   *   *

Sewing Ed's coat
Button upon it
for Bob to keep warm
in Amsterdam with Kev

Ed comes along
so three generations
With them and Fannie
who sewed other button

May they enjoy
the richness together
Me, babysitting Ella
Special time for us

May we all touch
the beauty and power
in ourselves and family
Sewing Ed's coat

18 January 2016

Jewish Museum visit
Sophie, Ella, Kev and I
Me wanting to share
ancestral connections
to help them with identity

Quilts of holocaust children
invited to Britain after war
Poignant, touching, inspiring
One with three generations now
says 'This is Ultimate Victory'

Playing immigrant board game
Us trying to get across
from *Shtetls* to England
Then Photos, talks of lives
as shop keepers, needle workers

Ella dresses in costume
as Yiddish theatre actress
Sophie taking in testimony
Children shot, people escape
to hide and live in forest

Girls sit at Friday night table
I say like their ancestors
It's women who light candles
Ella wants to eat fake Challah
There's laughter and joking

Ella hugs Sophie tightly
So good we've together
Three generation family
Kevin represents his
with thoughtfulness, smiles

Is it blood that defines us
culture or convictions?
Kids see Torahs, religious lives
Hear liberal Rabbi's opinion
and those of woman Rabbi

They say women are equal
encouraging past Orthodox
to listen, take in heritage
which they can interpret
in own way and time

This is what I wanted
beyond Bat Mitzvah or not
Broader view to encourage
process of developing
own realisations

Girls take up exhibit chalk
to answer blackboard queries
Who are you? What defines you?
And why does it matter?
Existential life questions

Sophie writes on the board
'I'm a 12 year old Jewish girl'
to what defines her – 'My family'
It matters 'because life and family
are amazing to be part of'

Ella's answer to all is
'I have Jewish blood family'
When asked as we leave
what thought of museum
both cousins reply, 'Cool'

On Holocaust Memorial Day
David Cameron dismisses refugees
as 'a bunch of migrants'
So sad and hurtful

Collective Responsibility
Waking in the night
to feel refugee's suffering
in my stomach and heart
How can I best help?

Anger at David Cameron
dismissing men, women, children
fleeing Syria, Iraq, Afghanistan
in Dunkirk, Calais mud 'jungle'
as 'a bunch of migrants'

'Swarms trying to break in'
he said of those risking lives
escaping violence we helped kindle
bringing families for safety
Wandering Europe this winter

He feeds fear, misperceptions
But don't want to feed my anger
It's not a lucid energy
Want to be clear-headed
to see what's best to do

In morning sunshine
Feet touching earth
Slowly solidity settles
and river flows on
Mother Nature heals

From there I can see
compassion begins with my
ancestral wounds triggered
of Jews from Russia, Poland
who also fled for refuge

Refuge starts in my heart
opening to warm light
transforming my hurt
with glow of understanding
that blossoms into kindness

Rippling out to all people
without a safe home
both here and abroad
May nectar of compassion
nurture you with ease

May we all touch our humanity
to live beyond fear's grasp
Including David Cameron
to awaken his own heart
to buried feel of caring

Seeing we're all effected
by suffering of dispossessed
we need to share our resources
Interdependent we have
Collective Responsibility

31 January 2016

Our hug on return
Bob's arms around me
hearts touching in warmth
Reunited after adventure

Went so well with Kevin
Amsterdam an old haunt
Experiencing together
energised, informed

So glad for culmination
of Bob's seventy-fifth
Successful momentum
to carry on with muse

I read start of new book
moved by his insights
With refugee ancestors
understanding more deeply

Spending afternoon with Ella
I tell her about book
Oh, she says, perceptively
'So I come from refugees'

Yes, in past people travelled
not stopped, as now, by borders
Queen Victoria let in everyone
wanting to come to these shores

Dressed in acting class tee shirt
Ella tells me what she's reading
how practicing singing, dancing
Sipping milkshake with delight

Grandma Rose would approve
used to give them to Mom
Thought too thin, needed it
Eat, *kinder*, nourishment

Ella's good at that
Today we have the food
Just *vant* us to be happy
I want to make the most of Now

Enriched by Bob, Kev link
sharing intellect, emotions
Kevin on great exploration
that PhD support allows

From film museum to Miro
they both mutually profit
I wrap in shawl they got
smile with their achievement

Knowing taking care of me
is the best for us all
Accepting my blessings
our hug on return

Being ancestor stream
through early ceremony
for year of the monkey
at Phouc and Phung's

From all generations
of my biological
spiritual antecedents
I miraculously arise

Of course, I am also
experiences of this life
surroundings, culture
collective consciousness

But these are interpreted
through ancestor meanings
Senses screened
with what's come before

Fear so very deep
back to Lizards and Jews
needing to flee
Be aware of hazards

Passing onto me
so I can watch out
but over-activated
keeping me from ease

Opening toward Oneness
I see fear's effects
Maybe I'll forget pin
passwords and lifelines

Manus so afraid
of this person letting go
Don't worry you'll be there
as part of beauty wholeness

Seeing how defensiveness
tightens delicate stomach
We need to take care of body
for this life to go on with you

I suddenly ask ancestors
'What if it's all my fault'
Practicing with no separate self
there is no problem

Then they say again
clearly so I can hear
'Ve just vant you to be happy'
Spiritual ancestors agree

Back into steps and breath
of Sangha concentration
I release to savour
being ancestor stream

*   *   *

As wind picks up
clouds cover sun
Gulls soar on currents
invisible to me

Still I can see
beauty in their flight
Water rippling below
on supersaturated land

This is my life
So glad to have it
Can hear Mom say
'Good to be out of hospital'

Enjoying for her
and dear sweet Dad
'You have no idea
how good to breathe fresh air'

Nearing my birthday
deepening no-death insight
Transformation brings healing
between Mom and I together

Opening to Mom's love
Allowing it through
Waves of affection
flowing for Joy

Of course she is in me
but obstacle of hurt child
blocked some of the light
of her warm caring

My inner transformation
allows for new conditions
Accepting her nurture
letting it through

After strange dream
Mom dying as plastic body
I try mouth to mouth
but I can't save her

More than Florence body
Yes, I do know that
Beyond my earlier grief
coming to new connection

There in my DNA
but so much more
Energy beyond space/time
waiting for when I'm ready

Slowly coming to it
more than her serenity
Depth of feelings for me
Opening to Mom's love

*   *   *

Electron potential
beyond particle or wave
Manifestation
of subject/object together

Quantum Physics
and also Buddhism
Produce same wisdom
from different angles

Thay's insights so clear
resonate inside me
into wider knowing
of no inner/outer

Beyond dualistic thinking
into Suchness of Universal
Ultimate Dimension
So happy to glimpse

Deep habit convictions
create energy vibrations
And what's drawn to them
effecting the future

*   *   *

Circular pattern
never exactly the same
yet not completely different
Just ever changing

Like little ones in park
Remembering granddaughters
Now Sophie almost teen
to become a Bat Mitzvah

And here am I
teaching Reiki Mindfulness
Completing the circle
with Thay, Usui Sensei

1 –2 March 2016

After dream of violence
Government chasing
into Turkish country
Adrenaline pumping

Find traditional people
Safe there for a bit
Lost contact with Bob
Suddenly eyes open

I'm back in my bed
Bob's snoring beside me
Shock and relief
Awakening into peace

Such a vivid dream
recalling what Thay said
Ancestors show us war
for understanding, compassion

What else can I do
Just gave to Save the Children
Slowly calming myself
Appreciating safe house

Drifting back to sleep
I find Bob again
That's better together
somehow we manage

Telling Bob this morning
He laughs at snoring comfort
Then gives me big hug
knowing what Thay meant

Our refugee ancestors
recognise this dream
from their realities
Flowing in our blood

How different day seems
This dark rainy morn
A wonder of security
compared to war zone

White swans on river
synchronising heads
Quiet non-danger
Just neighbour's vacuum

Doing what we can
Arrange produce pick up
for Foodcycle meal
Bob coming to help

*   *   *

Touching IMELDA action
women stand in the wind
arms linked across generations
Telling lives of unknown sisters

Forced to lie, flee to England
have backstreet abortions
with terrible consequence
of future infertility

Young rape victims
parents with malformed fetus
Daughters, grandmothers of Ireland
call their people to raise their voices

May warmth in Irish hearts
open to compassion
of women's right to choose
Touching IMELDA action

3 March 2016

MY BIRTHDAY

Turning 69
Do like the number
turned upside down
It is the same

Alignment, sync
balance, symmetry
Intertwined connection
through past, present, future

Dreamt this morning
sister came to wake me
'Happy Birthday
Dad's lox omelette's done'

Looked forward to see him
Of course, passed years ago
Sadness pours through
then realisation

He was ready to go
Room for new generations
Gave him Sophie baby photo
very happy great-grandchild

And I awaken to Bob
So here for me
with flowers and card
his love, big hug

Yesterday in half sleep
asked what I wanted
Enlightenment for me, Bob
and sake of all beings

Then need to keep growing
transforming difficulties
Saw braiding hair energies
with concentration

6 March 2016

Family Birthday Gathering
Uplifting, heartening
So enriching my life
with their loving presence

Each with own projects
interests, directions
Bringing them back here
to reconnect together

Eating *Kasha Varnishkes*
my favourite old taste
Introducing Helena to it
giving them take-home seeds

Walking Green with Mom, Dad
Reassuring they're still with me
flowing in blood to offspring
Dad's enthusiasm, Mom's serenity

Kevin busy exploring
deep in PhD thoughts
Off to foreign conferences
Us to watch Ella

Cousins reunite
and off they go
to have their secrets, fun
I enjoy their laughter

Kerin holding her own
with CPN in London
Church connection helpful
I release, wish her well

Bob brings in cake
Their song so warming
Sixty-nine with kin
Family Birthday Gathering

8 March 2016

GLIMPSES OF GREAT BRIGHT LIGHT

**Sent to advanced students
with termly announcement
of Reiki Share and courses**

Great Bright Light
state of awareness
Energy through
mind/body as one

Oneness connection
Dualism fades
into just being
True Self of Reiki

Wider and deeper
as we practice
Life as meditation
Mindfulness in daily life

Levels and stages
Building blocks support
steady pace, no rush
Attainment too is emptiness

Emptiness
No separate self
Feeling interconnection
Ease of resting there

Cosmic Interbeing
with natural flow
Buddhahood unfolds
Great Bright Light

*   *   *

Gradually in glimpses
more exposure occurs
from solid Hara base
building energy from practice

Sun within/without
shatters misperceptions
Releasing ego to become
Reiki rain without rainer

*   *   *

Just let Reiki rain
Frans Stiene advises
Let inner Buddha do it
Thay tells us again

So I come back
Practicing once more
Taking solid earth steps
Breathing Great Bright Light

Allowing myself
to remember true nature
There within smiling
radiating trust

From beauty perspective
of being the Oneness
Multicoloured tree trunks
restored to three dimensions

Whole brain working together
soliciting Manas
We need your help
in Watching with interest

You're most important
in transforming distraction
Valuing curious observing
in kindness and clarity

While still in bed
heard text come in
Thought would check weather
but answered text instead

Sure, Good I Noticed
But much more powerful
feeling the effects
of left brain on yoga

Ill-at-ease in morning space
My precious meditative time
Yoga, breakfast, walking, sitting
Building to mindful writing

Truly opening heart to Manas
You say do want inclusion
Seeing rejection reaction
built into childhood

*   *   *

Healing the 'Little Diddle'
Seeing self inflicting wounds
Mistaking that as loyalty
for what thought of as devilish

Family misperceptions
each based on own pain
Transferred to me
as a young child

Role no longer active
but reminisce remains
So glad I noticed
you cowering there

Time for transformation
way down at the base
So I release punishing
This person called Joy

Sending such kindness
understanding, embrace
Reiki back to little girl
What did I do wrong?

Distance healing for us all
Mom, Dad and Susan
Together within me
we can remake to Love

*   *   *

Hungry Ghost in dream
Hand of child wanting food
I bring, but grabs me instead
Arm stretches out as I run

Suddenly I scream
back into my bed
Bob shakes me saying,
'It's alright, I'm here with you'

Recalling caught sensation
of long arm holding me
Better than thought critique
to touch desire for true freedom

18 March 2016

NHS VULNERABILITY

Surprising vulnerable
at clinic appointment
Dermatology for my face
Somehow slipped off their list

Registrar wanted to see me
again after three months
but I only got appointment
one whole year later

Thought it was the cut backs
which shocked her and nurse
No, new computer system
just dropped off some people

They were apologetic
trying more tests and creams
Prescriptions to take to GP
But I felt somewhat shaken

I'm generally healthy
in control of own treatment
This exposed hidden fears
of my own fragility

Dear body I send you love
Reiki, wellbeing wishes
Realising your getting older
that this lifespan is limited

Stunned at deeper level
Brought out with Rosacea
Seborrhoeic Dermatitis
Registrar so kind, helpful

She's considered a junior doctor
in contention with government
over new contract they're imposing
Which BMA calls unsafe

Then there's Tory cutbacks
to disabled people
while cutting tax for wealthy
Which has me in a spin

Anger arising
Want to stop injustice
Breathing to perspective
Seeing impermanence

But so worrying for disabled
including my Loved-one
Clinic glimpse of how it feels
Perhaps that's what Osborne needs

Finding ways to campaign
Want to work with Labour
without getting tangled
in sectarian taking sides

Even some Tory MPs
still in touch with humanity
saying disabled cutbacks
are going too far

How many people
can government alienate
before their small majority
is suddenly shaken

Stepping back from worldly
to resonate compassion
for realisation we are all
Surprisingly vulnerable

23 March 2016

After yesterday in Brussels
seeing fear so pervasive
Collective consciousness
certainly effects mind

Isis attacks on people
sadness, compassion
Determination to respond
to hatred with love

Beautiful teacher article
of Muslim teens living
in poor area blamed
Wondering what did they do

Recommends befriending
Reconciliation
In Belgium and war zones
best weapon is love

Militarism feeds hatred
Dehumanisation
Education and jobs
feed integration

Aware collective consciousness
also has wondrous aspects
nourished by loving-kindness
over thousands of years

I choose these connections
over and again
through Reiki, meditation
mindfulness in daily life

Coming back to what Thay said
How each moment is a chance
to make peace with the world
The world needs our happiness

9 April 2016

Dancing at Sheila's memorial
as she would have liked
on dance floor she enjoyed
Zumba and whirling

Together once again
Brother's band plays
all the old songs
she liked to boogie to

Her energy so present
continuing with family, friends
Speaking of her caring
Activism for justice

From Student Occupations
Women's Liberation
to Brent Stop the War
Sheila brought the banner

Her organising skills
drive and persistence
for a fairer world
with peace and sharing

Sharing with her friends
our lives over decades
Dedication to family
Daughter, Mum, nieces, nephew

Her sister sends round book
for us to write remembrance
Won't forget that evening
Dear Sheila so pivotal

Affecting so many
her energy ripples out
in our actions and hearts
Dancing on with Sheila

Sophie's Bat Mitzvah
moving family event
Her connection to Jewish
heritage and ancestors

Reading out their names
Mom, Dad and Bob's
Us standing beside her
remembering grandparents

And back beyond
to those who fled Pale
All flowing anew
through Sophie's veins

May they protect her
nourish on journey
As family supports
holding hands and singing

Hevenu Shalom Aleichem
echoes as we walk round
this very special person
we bring Peace upon

Passed through millennia
I know they are happy
to see how their future grows
Flowering into womanhood

Marking age of responsibility
Sophie enters with strength
Developing her identities
Finding her own path

We all smile with love
touched by ceremony
Connection it empowers
in this remarkable young person

Amazed at her skill
for creative writing
kindness and inclusion
in time of confusion

All our love goes with you
on your right of passage
Joining Jews before you
Sophie's Bat Mitzvah

*   *   *

Freshness reverberating
after being with Ella
in London and here
Sharing enthusiasm

Taking her to school
meeting her new friend
wearing headscarf at ten
We say like its sparkles

Ella sparkles in many ways
plays guitar and sings
Researches cake recipes
she makes here with Bob

Chocolate, sugar, cream
Oreos in and topping
Taking to barbeque
Happy sharing her creation

Even interested in my crystals
I'm amazed how much I am
New Blue Bladed Kyanite
Clearing to what's important

It's this wondrous life
Breathing in morning chill
lucidity and light
Freshness reverberating

28 – 30 April 2016

WRITTEN FOR NEW MINDFULNESS LEVEL 2 COURSE

Circle of feelings
pleasant and painful
neutral and both
present at same time

As when Mom died
and afterwards I felt
intense depth of grief
surrounded by warm love

Knowing feelings come round
and that I'm so much more
Showing beauty to neutral ones
they smile in sun's glow

Cattle lie in abundant grass
Satisfied, chewing cud
In the moment, beyond knowing
summer's end brings their slaughter

When I stay with this lush field
resonating inside the Now
can smile to Manas bringing up
old dark feelings and memories

Yes, I understand
you want to stay in control
to safeguard the illusion
that I'm a separate self

Protecting this body
for this I am thankful
But you're also blind
to the wider vision

Seen from there, I laugh
transforming dread, fear
into freedom of earth step
This breath into wholeness

Suffering and Happiness
two sides of same coin
Metal in-between's
mindful awareness

That energy of Knowing
Perspective regained
Being Reiki resonating
through my whole body

Oh, what a *Machia*
such ease and comfort
Allowing green balance
to be restored again

Remember Brother saying
difficulty's good practice
Yes, I can see that
as my heart grows

Better able to live
at higher vibration
Practicing art of both
Suffering and Happiness

1 May 2016

ART OF SUFFERING (LESS)

The Art of Suffering
by not being caught
Not a victim of it
but creative transformations

Seeing hurt in heart
Kindness arises
also Find The Worst
but watching and knowing

Knowing I want to live
in way of Bodhicitta
The stream of compassion
for me and others

No need to be tangled
in peoples' misperceptions
I've enough of my own
that I'm slowly unravelling

In healing hurt, anger
from earlier memories
there's deeper transformation
Compassionate Detachment

Sending Reiki to us all
Stepping aside from ego
back to wider perspective
where true clarity returns

From there suffer so much less
allowing knots to pass
Walking deeply on Earth
She vibrates up energy

In times of confusion
Stability most needed
Keeping Heart opened
The Art of Suffering

4 May 2016

ART OF HAPPINESS

Art of Happiness
setting the intension
for Reiki to flow
in that direction

Feel it in my heart
as it opens wider
Embracing the pain
that still remains

It's in the noticing
that change occurs
Coming into bliss
deeper and fuller

Pleased for the growth
Unfurling like spring leaves
Allowing sweet process
of restoring life anew

Savouring the sunlight
Letting wind blow through
Blockages releasing
when conditions are right

Letting go to contentment
Focusing on the beauty
Such blessings of this day
More than enough

From earlier insight
Words trigger afresh
Life is so good
I am so Happy

Energy manifesting
Vibrating on Earth plane
Helping us all
Art of Happiness

5 May 2016

ACCEPTING BLESSINGS EXERCISE

Our idea of Happiness
may actually be an obstacle
Keeping us from being Happy
right now in this moment

What if we let go
of what we think we need
Look instead at what we have
Accepting Blessings Gratefully

Try making a list
of all the conditions
you already have
to be happy this instant

Here's the start of my list
Looking at it this way
I have more than enough
to just be happy right now

*   *   *

Appreciating my Blessings
more than I can number
Starting with my partner
Rippling out to wider family

This body in good health
Arms, feet to exercise
Walk on Mother Earth
into warm house of shelter

Then there's clean water
Miracle from the tap
As much as I want
for hot shower, tea

Thay and Usui Sensei
helping me to realise
this gratitude for all I have
Enjoying my Blessings

6 May 2016

*PLUM VILLAGE PLAN
WITH SOPHIE*

Accepting room placement
given us from New Hamlet
So want good trip for Sophie
and me to have some space

Sharing with two others
Earlier said mum and child
Don't exactly know now
but best to just let go

Remembering visit
years ago with whole family
When all I could do then
was trust and let it be

Yes, it worked out well
always has at Plum Village
No point in ringing them again
and be caught in complications

Thay says it our misperceptions
of ourselves and others
that causes fear, misunderstanding
So I'll just accept and smile

Tilling fields of Mind
my true occupation
Planting seeds of kindness
Weeding out Find The Worst

On compost heap
you can transform
into new growth
Beyond binding tangles

Transformations now
ripple on to future
projects and family
Sophie, me on Retreat

17 May 2016

Waiting for Thay in hospital
Searching for him there
Awakening from dream
Now he walks with me by river

Water rippling past
rolling on irrespective
of passing disturbance
Grateful not noise of bombs

Once heard Thay say
that even as bombs fell
he could notice rhythm
of sounds they made

As a Brooklyn kid
raised in city cement
couldn't have imagined
stepping out door to river

But here we are by current
vivid beauty of flow
Nirvana of just being
Oneness with nature

*   *   *

Remembering how nun told us
she always cried when meditating
Thay said she'd have so much energy
once she'd transformed the sadness

Witnessing that truth in her
now that she'd done the work
Her smile, glow and wisdom
present for us to profit

Yiddishe energy
rising up from ancestors
Feeling it through me
Relaxing to Brooklyn accent

There such great warmth
arms spread so wide
to wrap around me
in loving embrace

Sure, there was angst
Oy gevalt again
the chosen people
Victims of Holocaust

Born right after that
seeing numbers on arms
And Jewish Americans
with the guilt and fear

Stay in the ghetto
safer from anti-Semitism
OK, Southern Italians
our cultures simpatico

School overcrowded
Couldn't learn to read
Just another bulge baby
far too many of us

My parents meant well
though had own problems
But Mom so wanted
us to have happy childhood

In Brooklyn one bed flat
Parents slept on fold-out couch
so we could have the bedroom
with more space to play

As they grew older
moving to Newark
Building their confidence
Exploring the arts

Mom as Girls Scout leader
such a model for me
Them taking up oil painting
Us enjoying museums

I fit in less in Newark
though walked through storm
with head up high
Finding my own way out

It's only now I'm older
mindfully watching what comes
that can truly befriend
the fear of Evil Eye

Don't be too happy
you'll pay for it later
That old default setting
Oy gevalt what next?

Glad I comprehend
ancestors want me happy
So that I can release
ancient ghetto mentality

Opening my heart
to receive their energy
of strength and endurance
Transforming our difficulties

From this perspective
of wider understanding
can make good use of
Yiddishe energy

23 May 2016

24 May 2016

Dwelling in Nirvana
in glimpses on Green
After bad night's sleep
such a welcomed relief

Loved-one's visits
not always easy
for her or for us
Then I get caught

Nirvana's extinction
of misperceptions
creating such suffering
as my mind tangles

So much more difficult
to be skilful from that place
Reiki teaching brought me back
to wider perspective

Returning to awareness
What a great relief
From there I can have
compassion for us all

Starting with myself
Seeing guilt, fear
for Loved-one in distress
Life's confusing for her

Wishing Loved-one well
on her own journey
knowing I can't save her
as it's her voyage

But when I take care
of this person called Joy
I can have more patience
for her when she visits

Wild garden freedom
as with my heart
Allowing perennials
to bloom with the sun

Cutting away high grass
of old pain and sorrows
Letting mindful kindness
bring transformation

Fresh rejuvenation
of I know not what
Think it's orange flowers
but will just have to see

Still I am holding you
life Koan of Loved-one
in the breezy beauty
of sunlight and spring

We grow together
in understanding energy
of endurance opportunities
to practice anew

May seeds of compassion
watered by teardrops
bring forth true happiness
for me and daughter

And may they spread
carried by winds of caring
to grow all over planet in
Wild garden freedom

14 June 2016

FOR DEAR DIANA ARONSTAM

Dear Diana, old friend
your energy lives on
in all of us you touched
Students, colleagues like me

Remembering many years ago
when we met at Kilburn College
Your dedication to Outreach Course
you ran on difficult Estate

In my first year as part-timer
you offered me work there
I accepted, then was warned
it was a dangerous place

So you said you'd drive me
and did so each week
to have English teacher
for women there so grateful

Your course meant so much to them
Your extra time, skills you offered
And through our weekly rides
you and I became friends

Then when I was nervous
before my college job interview
you told me you enjoyed yours
'A chance to tell them what I thought'

Your vision and drive
for True Education
for those who need it so much
was a real inspiration

What you said gave me confidence
Support to follow convictions
Your energy of really caring
carries on through many teachers

Your work helping students
have a better life chance
continues in each of them
and all the work they do

Sad you've passed away
but glad you went peacefully
I planted bulbs in front garden
where you and Kathy visited

When flowers bloom each year
I'll think of you and generations
of students and colleagues
Blossoming anew

Your energy ripples on
through all of us you influenced
for Education with Justice
An equal chance for everyone

Beautiful flowers'll spring forth
each summer with this energy
of dedication, skill and caring
you've left us, Dear Diana

15 June 2016

CULTIVATING EU STABILITY

Cultivating Solid Stability
in time of rising fears
of European break-up
Xenophobia

Talking to other voters
of how we're interconnected
as one European Community
to see our mutual interests

Revisiting terrible wars
that ravaged this continent
in the twentieth century
EU has helped prevent more

In just a few days
Britain has a vote
which could take us away
from all we've jointly gained

The Social Chapter
better workers' rights
maternity benefits
protection for part-timers

Humanitarian safeties
No Death Penalty
Societal Freedoms
of press, speech to join

Doing what I can
canvassing, leafleting
Putting up signs
Voter registration

Polls say Leave will win
but it's so very close
just keep doing my best
Cultivating Solid Stability

17 June 2016

FOR JO COX MURDERED MP

Uniting against Hatred
with energy of Compassion
Bathing her children in love
as Brendan Cox said

You were a light
of caring for others
Opening your heart to
refugees and migrants

In touch with your humanity
you could connect with theirs
Through Oxfam then as MP
to stay linked with Europe

Supporting Yorkshire communities
against austerity cuts
that push more into poverty
Let's share the wealth instead

Flying IN flag with flotilla
on boat with children, husband
Just the other day
on great family outing

Never suspecting
as none of us did
On way to constituency surgery
you would be shot dead

Witnesses say he shouted
'Put Britain First'
Hatred and delusion
turned against your kindness

Such sadness for us all
to lose you so young, Jo
But we pick up your torch
and carry on your light

18 June 2016   22 June 2016

REFERENDUM TRANSFORMATIONS

In time of controversy
of EU Referendum
Fear breading Xenophobia
Finding Flower Freshness

Practicing with Sangha
children and parents
at Mini Day of Mindfulness
I'm happy to facilitate

Bringing crocheted flower
attached upon a stick
She's friend of Tiger puppet
that the children call Smile

We practice with the sound
of the bell we pass round
Feeling Flower in heart centre
Sitting with Freshness energy

Then I take kids to the park
so parents have half-hour sit
Laughing, climbing, playing
They take turns with the puppet

Years ago bought for my kids
grown as old as their parents
We talk of baby pictures
There's new generation wonder

Returning home it's easier
to ripple out their inclusiveness
from mixed origins and races
they only see each other as friends

Transforming my defensiveness
Nurturing deeper understanding
where love blooms togetherness
into fresh flower of sharing

I want to ripple caring
to all those in pain
from this referendum
bringing division and worry

Much of it's misplaced
onto European Union
I open my heart
to all who are scared

After leafleting I felt
vulnerability arising
Experiencing hostility
from some who disagreed

Mostly they were men
with so much anger inside
feeling working class suppression
Venting some on a woman

Of course there were others
confused and undecided
that I could talk with
about no more wars in Europe

As Phouc said at Sangha
after Vietnam War
the most important thing
is not to have anymore

Community within me
embracing defensiveness
sense of 'self' needing protection
We will take good care of you

In the transformation
of old and new hurt
the energy'll be available
to go canvassing tonight

24 & 25 June 2016

REMAIN LOSS

Remain loss
Shock, Horror
Slowly sinking in
as heard first vote totals

Hopeful earlier
as polls said close win
Did Tellings with big turnout
thought to be good sign

Remain would be great relief
Able to got back to normal
After months of building tension
activism and sorrow

Jo Cox's tragic death
Leave stoking Xenophobia
I kept coming back to practice
Walking slowly by the river

Now the worst has happened
I stop to breathe with church bells
Appreciating vivid moments
like resting next to Bob

Both of us up late
Final results this morning
Not wanting to be wound-up
by hearing any more news

Instead watching clouds pass
fluffy against blue sky
as Bob sleeps beside me
I am so grateful

In time of uncertainty
returning to Earth stability
Sharing with Kev on phone
He wants compassionate society

Yes, but must begin
with compassion for ourselves
Embracing the pain
to heal and ripple out

Connecting with Helena
says school parents devastated
in multicultural playground
Depressed and confused

Helena, Kevin determined
It's the fight of our lives
for Britain we want to live in
Daughter having diverse friends

Our family united
Kerin texted had voted
just before polls closed
She wanted us to know

*   *   *

Compassionate embrace
of frustration feelings
Anger, disempowerment
Tangles of confusion

Tragedy compounded
as will hurt Leave voters
Many poor austerity victims
voted 'take back control'

So misleading and untrue
this would give them comfort
Not immigrants, but government
who has instituted brutal cuts

We don't know exactly
what will be negotiated
Not even who will do that
We'll struggle on for human rights

26 June 2016

Practicing Reiki Precepts
in time of great turmoil
In the Here and Now
Brings me back to Earth

Settling from mind spin
of Referendum defeat
Signing new petitions
Passing them on

On river's other shore
water lilies float steadily
Boats cause waves upon them
but they're rooted deep in mud

Mud of my worry
What will happen next
Uncertainty, disappointment
Fear for the future

Sister Annabel reminds
Lotuses need mud
to nourish rejuvenate
their growth for fresh buds

Remembering to come back
down from head to feet
Seeing what arises
Let anger pass mindfully

Yes, you are there
No need to judge
Breathing and watching
Embracing hurt with kindness

We're caught up in the tumult
Collective Consciousness Energy
May Earth energy of solidity
help us ground to lucidity

27 June 2016

Healing into Nirvana
Even just partially
Allowing myself to be here
as much as I can

Healing into the present
Despair surrounded by beauty
Tall grass seeds swaying
in gentle wind on Green

Cattle munching them up
Together cycle complete
with cow patty right by hoof
This person witnesses it all

In vividness of needing
clarity this instant
Transforming, rejuvenating
back to Nirvana

    *   *   *

Heron appears on shore
peering into depths of water
Angler throws him tiny fish
still flapping heron swallows it

Who's side am I on?
Fish or heron, I wonder
Then realize there's no divisions
No need to choose one against other

Wanting this same vision for
UK EU citizens and Leave voters
Many of us worried, confused
by this uncertainty unleashed

Lots of us who worked so hard
for Remain vote, now dashed
Embracing unknown with Knowing
If not part of problem, not in solution

After night of long knives
against elected Labour Leader
When Kevin, Helena, Ella
stood in Parliament Square
with 10,000 supporters
there to protect, defend him

They say that Jeremy is spineless
but withstood such personal abuse
in a coup designed to topple him
Rather than follow agreed
procedure for leadership election
and not split the Labour Party

They say he's unelectable
yet so many Leave voters
now say they did it as a protest
against establishment politicians
which Corbyn is certainly not
instead for peace, human rights
He'd defend in Brexit talks

After Remain defeat
this instability which follows
from markets and business
some already making layoffs
This country is rocked, divided
from unnecessary referendum

At this time of unsteadiness
which I too can be caught up in
I come back to breath and body
Doing deep relaxation
at 5am when awakened
by mind spin, adrenaline

*   *   *

After walk on the Green
Pouring sorrows out to river
She receives and rolls on
back to the sea

Why did Leave win?
Why have a referendum?
Oh, yes, Second Arrow
of what's already happened

Enjoying the cattle
grazing in far pasture
Seeing their ease
Not knowing of future

Neither do I, of course
though imagining brings worry
Not healthy for my body
Noticing, return to summer's day

Polish houseboat neighbour
passes with her toddler
I smile, greet her warmly
She appreciates in this uncertainty

It's people like her family
who've come to work, settle here
Suddenly so vulnerable
in toxic atmosphere of suspicion

I wave to baby who grins
opening my heart
Yes, it is a happy moment
Storing up for what's to come

29 June 2016

The agony continues
but so does my practice
So thankful for that
What would I do without it?

Helena was told yesterday
by another school parent
to go back to Ireland
as he gloated as UKIP voter

She said, We built this country
and were granted right of abode
not connected with the EU
How dare you say that

His daughter, half Filipino
is a good friend of Ella's
She and another friend
had convinced her for Remain

The other friend's Mum said
when he came over talking glad
that she didn't want to speak of it
but he just kept going on

They ended up answering back
that's when he told other Mum
If you don't like it here
you should move to Scotland

Afterwards both Mums
decided to tell the office
Not wanting anything done
but just to have it logged

School took it seriously
Other Mum broke into tears
connecting with her ancestors
who were refugees

Women felt as white, educated
they could hold their own
But were more concerned for
the ethnic minority parents

I know the guy who said this
He's a London bus driver
White working class, oppressed
Wanting to take back control

Enormous contradictions
with his Filipino wife
They've a disabled son
Were given council housing

Of course, Helena still wants
Ella to play with his daughter
who may face discrimination
in this time of rising racism

Reports are coming in
of increase since Leave victory
Then there's MPs vote against
Jeremy Corbyn, elected leader

Yesterday I clicked and signed
emailed everything I could
Now I just need some space
to recover and recuperate

The future's more uncertain
than it normally seems
Though everything changes
it's not usually this dramatic

When I let go of 'I'
so much less to defend
Taking weight off shoulders
that I'm somehow responsible

1 July 2016

Kindly watching what arises
Trusting, allowing it up
from Store so very deep
where memories, potentials lie

And what I see seems surprising
The earnestness of survivor guilt
That I didn't die in the holocaust
Family escaped to States instead

Then raised to blame the Germans
who sat by, let the Jews be killed
So we were taught to speak out
or else responsible for genocide

That's what propelled my action
against the Vietnam War
Burned baby leaflets grabbed
balled up, thrown in our faces

Of course, that was early on
Later mass movement shifted tide
But post-Brexit vote brings me back
to the great need for anti-racism

Oh, the Collective Consciousness
in such turmoil on these islands
In state of fear, misperceptions
Hate crime increase after vote

By fivefold the police now say
No, I just want this to stop
Not blaming, not letting it happen
But I'm not in control

Nor am I directly responsible
needing to carry on shoulders
Without it I'm freer to see
what best to do and not do

2 July 2016

Holding Wandering Jew
with kindness, understanding
Scared seed reinforced within
for so many generations

Energy of strength and love
coming up, embracing to support
the sadness, grief and tears
of being an 'outsider' again

Vote watering divisions
Those who are 'British' and not
More than passport, an ethnicity
Craving back to isolation

The unity of being European
with diversity, as well as problems
is so much more inclusive
Even Wandering Jew can join

*　　　*　　　*

Depression is anger turned inward
Realisation coming back again
Anger at vote and confusion
Anger at me, who couldn't stop it

Such tangles in my mind
I kept arguing back through
Feeding dissolution more
with 'why' of Second Arrow

Letting it go, now that I can see
root of despair that kept arising
Discovering with eyes that recognise
Depression is anger turned inward

3 July 2016

The gladiolas are coming up
that I planted for dear Diana
after she peacefully passed
Then planted more for Jo Cox
after her tragic murder

Seemed a fitting way
to feed transformation
Holding grief with love
the hope of life cycle
blossoming anew again

But in gloom that's followed
the vote to leave EU
depression and sorrow
Xenophobia stirred up
Rain and hale poured down

With a sense of despair
I gave up on the bulbs
Thought maybe next year
when conditions were better
they might rise from depths

Peaceful walking on Green
giving myself a break
from all the bad news
Stepping between cow shit
Geez, so much fertiliser

Cheering myself up
as rally did for Corbyn
Coming back to blessed house
then suddenly I notice
The gladiolas are coming up

5 July 2016

After Diana's funeral
Old colleagues, more recent
gather for her send off
connecting with her memory

Going with Kev, Helena
Her part of all our work
Giving teaching to Helena
who said how learnt from her

Finding out more about Diana
who'd touched all our lives
Commitment to helping students
Her fight for just education

Passing at age fifty-seven
I wonder at what she'd missed
What was her internal dimension
So glad that she had Dennis

Also knew him from college
and again got to see Kathy
who taken Diana to Chemo
Been such a close friend

Reconnecting to that time
twenty-five years ago
Kathy helped me at Kilburn
when I really needed a job

Our families became friends
Kevin was only eleven
just about Ella's age now
We went to Terry's PhD party

Now Kev's working on his
that's how the circle turns
Life, Death, Continuation
Savouring being alive

6 July 2016

Speaking out against injustice
Thay says part of our practice
Since Brexit, rise of racism
How can we best transform it?

A friend on Northern tram
witnessed group of white men
shout 'Paki' at Asian woman
Friend apologised when men left

A middle class English dad
just told a school parent
that Hitler wasn't all wrong
about what he said of Jews

My son and daughter-in-law
along with other school parents
asking Head to write to all
saying hate crimes not tolerated

They are meeting to support
their multicultural community
with its beauty of London diversity
Building on children's friendships

What can we do as a Sangha?
First starting with ourselves
I've been walking by river
healing my hurt, despair

Sister Annabel was asked
at Miracle of Mindfulness retreat
How can we support refugees
and migrants in our communities

She said bring issues to Sangha
as many eyes gain perspective
Ask if other Sangha members
might like to join in a project

7 July 2016

Talked to Sangha last night
about how we can respond
to racism, xenophobia
Good discussion, will send petition

Now need to release tangles
Don't have to have opinion
on every twist and turn
the News puts out to entice

Yes, there's things to do
but not at this moment
I'm supposed to be on holiday
Now that Reiki classes ended

After Diana's funeral
powerful realisation
that this is only time
to build aware inner life

Inner/out illusion
yet need to start here
Where pain/sorrow manifests
awaiting transformation

And I am here for you
in turbulent times
Feet vibrating Earth
flowing up body

Ploughing field of mind
Releasing heart centre
My true occupation
best for me and all

And from that solidity
with chest-broad expanse
watching Cygnets grow
Letting go to summer

9 July 2016

Release of Chilcot report
Held back for many years
Tells of Blair's misdeeds
No real need for Iraq War

Transforming darkness
Apology for Iraq War
by Jeremy Corbyn
leader of Labour Party

Touching for so many
Families of Iraqis
Solders killed in fighting
All of us who opposed it

You spoke against war, Jeremy
Scorned in parliament then, now
But still focused with persistence
of desire for peace and justice

So needed in this country
torn apart by Brexit
May clarity of Interbeing
bring us back together

*   *   *

Transforming darkness
Thay practiced through long war
Touching spirit of his Sangha
with a heart needing peace

Suffering of Vietnam War
Iraqi one more recent
Fear of another Europe war
Can be seen with wider vision

In our troubled times
here in the UK
birdsong still penetrates
to depths of my being

10 July 2016

Old friend cycles by
stops to talk of turmoil
World turned upside down
by Brexit, shifting politics

Yes, I've felt that too
But came back to tree roots
I point to large steady one
and leaves that sway in storm

She wants to return
to what's really important
But news revelations
keep changing our world

That is also true
but I've stopped watching TV
Just creating inner turmoil
when I need to stay steady

Finding out main news
and signing petitions
But still able to appreciate
the beauty of this summer

She agrees there's collective energy
Wants to be stable one in it
Yes, that's a way to influence
and I've shifted focus to that

*   *   *

Reiki yesterday with Liz
so helpful to letting go
of built-up defensiveness
Blocked energy released

Giving each other treatments
Sharing our practice together
How dealt with Leave result
Watching feelings, embracing

11 July late evening & 12 July morning 2016

Coming as realisation
Vision of Ultimate energy
manifesting into white form
that I saw was me

I am the Ultimate
manifesting as Joy
Just as the ocean
manifests waves

Creating particular shape
based on conditions
Like amount of wind
salt content of water

This manifestation shape
is based on ancestors
experience, environment
spiritual energy, karmic action

Nothing to search for
because Ultimate is perfect
and I contain it all
Beyond dualistic illusions

So what is there to fear
when I can't be lost, destroyed
Nothing to gain that isn't here
already in this enactment

Such a realisation
I've known all along
Yet insight vision
suddenly made clearer

What do I do now?
Just relax and be
Letting go of attainment
Enjoying who I really am

May I keep this clarity
by feeding it with practice
Watching habit energies
with Ultimate vision

Everyone is Ultimate
everything around me
In beauty of connection
Oneness so evident

Arising anew each instant
in vivid impermanence
There is fresh potential
to let go of the past

I can just see Thay
motioning with his hand
'Just keep letting go
letting go, letting go'

Sitting by the river
in newness of morning
Water runs through heart
washing away grief

Yes, worries for future
release in this second
Seeing fear and happiness
both come from the mind

In re-creation freshness
possibility in this Now
I enjoy new wonder of
Manifesting from Ultimate

25 – 28 July 2016

PLUM VILLAGE WITH SOPHIE

Mind shift phenomenal
just what I needed
This Collective Consciousness
What a mindful difference

Outstretched fields
vineyards, sunflowers
Wonder of pink sunrise
walking to meditation

*　　　*　　　*

Practice continuation
walking again with Thay
Him now in wheelchair
Sangha walks for him, us

No separation
Stepping with his feet
He looks at me with presence
half-smiling as we bow

My heart opened by chanting
So touched by reconnection
Seeing him again
though often feel him in me

*　　　*　　　*

Sophie, so glad
that you've connected
with healing elements
of Plum Village

To be able to practice
with your teen friends
Sharing, transforming
with your own Sangha

Her off with them now
I relax in the shade
of cornfield surround heat
after deep Dharma Talk

*　　　*　　　*

Plum Village together
Sophie and I
Wonder, adventure
experience of growth

Each on own programme
Her exploration with teens
Both of us like to walk
alone in Plum Orchard

Sophie tells me a saying
I just have to smile
'Be yourself
everyone else is taken'

We are each like that
in our own ways
Accepting Sophie's beauty
being as she is now

Teen years not easy
I remember my confusion
Giving her space, privacy
while still being there for her

Being here for me
My healing, self-love
Best way to support us
Plum Village together

NOTES ON THE 5TH MINDFULNESS TRAINING FOR PLUM VILLAGE PANEL

Mindful Consumption
safety of awareness
Guarding my consciousness
to support profound fear

Wanted Five Trainings
to deepen concentration
See what prevents that
so can know what to do

Trainings as a guide
to move in right direction
Like following North Star
if you want to head north

Not taken as commandments
Don't want sin/guilt trap
Can already give me hard time
without need for anymore

So what are these pollutants
Distractions so appealing
like Internet searching
What am I really looking for?

This feeling of longing
Good, I see you there
It's not info I need
but understanding

Better to sit
walk gently on earth
Mind untangles
enabling clarity

What I find is turmoil
in me, collective consciousness
from Brexit shock waves
turning world upside-down

Withdrawing from TV news
Guarding what I read
Only enough info
to basically keep up

Even if I don't
not really important
Better to shift energy
to compassion for all

May Peace of this retreat
ripple back with me to UK
where harmony's so needed
Loving-kindness for the world

*   *   *

Seeing Sister Insight
finger on lips
Shhhh, Shhhh, Joy
Motioning to brain

Then she smiled
and I did the same
Taking her advice
for 5th MT talk

With clarity of mind
could hear other panellists
Not practicing in brain
Nor reading my notes

Left poem in pocket
Let words come from Store
Trusting, immersed in
Plum Village energy

3 - 9 August 2016

AFTER READING NEXT PAGE OF THAY'S INSIDE THE NOW

The Here and Now
joined in present
Seeing, being in
Historical Dimension

Shock of this instant
can almost be to much
Stopping, relaxing
Just sun through leaf shade

River ripples sparkle
Breathing down to Earth
Stepping gently upon her
as soft breeze washes through

Sound of leaf song
Wind rustling branches
Dancing and swaying
as trunk stands so still

Feeling that steadiness
deep in this person
At home dwelling in
the Here and Now

*   *   *

One hundred little monkey
allergy patch tests on back
Taken off, nothing found
Back Monday to check

But what did happen
was connection to nurse
Teaching her mindful walking
Wants to pass on to patients

How wondrous she found
watching breath, earth link
NHS now so stressful
Eczema patients feel the same

For me the acceptance
of face spots and redness
as part of my practice
Nothing's seriously wrong

Still I'd like solution
to what body's telling me
Not yet discovered
though new diet helps

Connecting with women
waiting for blood tests
Dementia of one's husband
Other worried, hospitalised

So lucky that I'm healthy
To send compassion to them
Must begin with myself
Allowing kindness through

*   *   *

Builders' noise again
But can Touch the Earth
Letting go upon her
angst and turmoil

Neighbour's ladders
overlooking Mindful Eating
Still I feel the gift
of Universe's sustenance

Father and son
fixing next door
Respect their work
skill and humanity

Releasing back to Earth
her vibration rises through me
Healing and nurturing
in the Here and Now

13 August 2016

Absorbing shock waves
Staying fresh and solid
After Loved-one missing
Found in mental hospital

Keeping herself safe
best thing to do
But for us so worrying
when we couldn't find her

Hospital much better
than other fears
Slowly subsiding
with energy of compassion

Compassion for Loved-one
me and whole family
Sadness for illness
that brought her to A&E

Not easy for us all
Seeing this in me
But glad I got to talk to her
Tell her we all love her

Now the residuals
Meeting CPN, doctor
Setting up a plan
She needs more support

So dreaded this happening
Yet not how I expected
Didn't feel like last time
Twelve years ago

Backdrop of worst fears
put it all in proportion
Lot's of ideas to help her
But need to start with myself

17 August 2016

Healing once again
accepting, transforming
Loved-one's breakdown
Here within myself

Her great move to London
Now seems in disarray
But feeding cat, cleaning flat
It's all there when she's ready

But breakdown so sad
Seeing her like that
I took off my hoodie
She wrapped herself in it

On the other hand, she's safe
Own room, being cared for
Needs a space to recuperate
Not have to deal with life

Gave her Sophie's card
photos of her, family
She did smile when heard
girls played in sprinkler park

All I can really do
is embrace my sorrow
Holding my heart
Healing once again

26 August 2016

Embracing night fears
Preparing to visit
Loved-one in hospital

But first this day of peace
Nurtured by the beauty
of river, life with Bob

Nearly 50 years together
through difficulty, romance
All part of the adventure

Like on motorcycle trip
camping, exploring Europe
Before having children

I read him Pema Chodron's
When Things Fall Apart
A different way of seeing

We both agree possible
Certainly not easy
Though no way, but to grow

Fruits of unwanted hells
are also very useful
Sweet in their own way

We hug, connect hearts
Going on together
Our love will see us through

29 August 2016

After such spin of visit
to Loved-one in hospital
Walking by the river
finally calming mind

Then at Sangha sit
quietly crying
Releasing to collective
healing vibration

There for each other
OI sisters and brothers
Walking on Thay's path
making it our own

Returning to energy
of Plum Village stay
Brother said bathe in it
Take it back with you

Yes, I have done that
and needed it so much
Preparing to enter
mental health ward

Sleepless night followed
such endless mind spin
Every time I'd relax
thinking flooded back

Sangha kindness helped
sitting in Jane's garden
Peacefully together
slowly healing heart

So I rise back up
from the depths again
Savouring summer's day
Reset to Now reality

31 August - 3 September 2016

Flowers bloom from depths
for dear Diana and I
Planted in early summer
Commemorating her life

Never knowing what onset
of this season would bring
But still they blossom up
through nurturing earth

Planting's what I could do
in so many forms
Poetry and bulbs
Flourishing of beauty

It's there all the time
like sun behind clouds
Opening to your light
Flowers bloom from depths

*   *   *

Known at deeper level
this unknown I step into
Vibrating with life force
Mind of love Reiki

This Heart, Mind as one
No separation anywhere
What Manas truly wants to preserve
is way beyond this person

Oh, this sweet kindness
Mother Nature's embrace
Energy Mom called God
So complete and healing

Expanding these months
as I do, as well
Through happiness, difficulties
Known at deeper level

*   *   *

Insight of mind projection
Seeing what you really are
Notions of the future
that don't actually exist

Plum Village collective energy
still resonating right now
within and manifesting
when I tune into it

Sure there's pain, as well
but nothing wrong with that
Soothing you with compassion
from inside/outside

*   *   *

Holding heartbreak
with kind attention
In nature's embrace
out on the Green

Feeling my sorrow
Pain so very deep
Showing it the beauty
of leaves against blue sky

Staying with the moment
best that I can
Drifting into mind projection
then coming back to now

Over and over
That's what I can do
Stepping on the Earth
with concentration

Slowly relief comes
Letting go of tangles
So that my heartbreak
breaks my heart open

Walking old path
of Faire and Spirit
Coming back again
to practice for healing

Waking in the night
Mind-spin and sadness
Guilt and reproach
What can I do?

Know I can't save her
yet such pain for Loved-one
Here in my heart
closing it down

Writing notes in darkness
of what I need do
Don't forget this and that
as if that would solve it

This morning on Common
coming back to nature
Stourbridge Faire History
Newton bought first prism

Paths then as well
as for spiritual ancestors
Walking on the Earth
with footsteps of peace

*　　*　　*

Old friend dear Manas
As I get to know you
Seeing how your grasping
keeps me awake at night

Way back to childhood
not wanting to let go
Safer to be alert
then surrender to sleep

Thank you old friend
for all your protection
But you're misguided
Oneness is beyond fear

In opening to release
there's safety in surrender
Beyond judgement to wholeness
of life's ebb and flow

We're not really in charge
but just a wave through time
space and life force
ever flowing, changing

What a relief
much better that way
Can't save Loved-one
but can emanate blessings

Only from clearer place
am I able to do that
So please support
old patterns to fall away

If you'd like to continue
as part of 'Joy' person
You need to assist
release of negative habits

Though built-up through lifetime
you also have greater knowing
of clear consciousness below
which we manifest out of

Let's return there together
all aspects of this person
to bask in the healing
Nourishment to carry on

14 September 2016

After hearing Eckhart Tolle

Accepting the unacceptable
is first step to change
Surrendering to the Now
Its beauty and pain as one
In that Oneness of melding
comes alchemy of transformation

The clarity of Serenity
Mom found and said
Kerin needs to find herself
May her suffering be great teacher
that leads her to Now peace

Me accepting that she's suffering
but I don't really know how much
That she's being looked after
is safe, fed, getting meds
I can dwell more in mindfulness
allow blooming of true compassion

Compassionate Detachment
for my pain and hers
Seeing it in perspective
Calming, letting go
In the flow of release
happiness is possible

May my happiness blossom
with heart flower wide
Returning to Earth's healing
Reiki naturally ripples through
continuing out to loved-ones
the Universe and back

From there I can see
misperception of judgement
toward myself and daughter
Block of fear that colours
my vision to reject life
as unacceptable, which I accept

16 September 2016

Shifting once again
weather and Loved-one
Agreeing to be moved
to Recovery Ward

Starting to improve
So thankful for that
Letting life flow through
as stream continues

So many generations
emotions through time
Ancient Amber tree resin
glows orange in the sun

As Labradorite reflects light
I feel its encouraging
vibration to trust my
abilities and intuition

Returning to wider vision
Heart reopens with kindness
crystals and compassion
for me, Bob, daughter

Giving her space
Sending good wishes
She wants a time to rest
recuperate and heal

Clearly that's best
Not only can't I save her
but even if I could
it'd ruin her chance to grow

Back to Nirvana ease
Lapis Lazuli energy
So soothing and healing
Shifting once again

22 September 2016

Crying in far field
Asking Mom for help
Releasing back to Earth
after visiting Loved-one

Not what expected
Know it never is
Did what I could
May she be well, healthy

Day before prepared
possibility wouldn't see me
or have me meet doctor
Accepted best I could

But she had shifted
I gave her photos, chocolate
We just talked briefly
Met doctor on my own

Explained best I could
Difficulties she's always had
They won't call it autism
but helpful to understand her

Told I'm going away
on long-planned holiday
Gave Kevin's phone number
Will meet again when return

Taking days to recover
unwind and let go
So grateful for Bob's love
hugs and my practice

So I walk on the grass
stepping with my breath
out with the cattle
Crying in far field

23 September 2016

Know I need the respite
after summer difficulties
Loved-one's breakdown, Brexit
Now have to recuperate

Have done everything I could
to ensure her three weeks
are possibility for healing
The rest is up to her

She doesn't even want me
to do anymore
Wants independence
even if she's unwell

Later she may want my help
and I need to be in best place
to be able to do that mindfully
So first there's this holiday

Back to Salema
restful rejuvenation
Swimming and laughing
Bob and I together

Happiness is best antidote
May mine ripple out to you
dear daughter in difficulty
May your spirit rise anew

See you on my return
Now we each need space
I walk, breathe in beauty
Gently smiling in far field

28 September 2016

SALEMA HEALING

Sea flowing through
ripples of mind
Clearing again
back to the flow

There I can find you
Ease of eye roll back
into my brain
Softening to wellness

Difficulties fade
reverting to proportion
Seeing once again
My healing's best for all

Regaining wisdom
Can only save myself
Don't even know
what Loved-one's doing now

Her suffering's potential
for such transform
Trusting her true nature
to guide her to other shore

Just letting it all go
Mountains of misperceptions
pulverised back to sand
by centuries of waves

In this respite space
Allowing us the time
to each have ways of healing
Return to Salema Magic

3 – 4 October 2016

SALEMA SHANA TOVA

The gift is life
This 5777
New Year, new start
to bloom, transform

How many generations
of life stories on this beach
And I have opportunity
to add mine of growth

As I bask in rock's shade
savouring cosmic offering
of bread and cheese
Digesting sea's beauty

I know I can do it
Release difficulties
to be his fresh start
The gift is life

*   *   *

Shana Tova
A goten yer
Singing with old friends
A *Yiddishe* fest

New Year's resolution
Be kinder to fear, worry
Smile of Notice earlier
Embrace in awareness

Broad as sea flow
sunlight reflecting
warmth of understanding
Holding *de Kindela*

There in tender arms
of Mama support
Compassion so wide
Shana Tova

7 October 2016

Figueira return
Again to the source
of river coming back
once more to the sea

Drawn to revisit
through valley of growth
vineyards, tomatoes
cork and fig trees

Stepping gently on earth's
path through wild herbs
So reminiscent
Lush and fresh

Viewing beyond
where mountains part
Sea sparkles ripple
beckoning us on

Across river rocks
we support each other
Then down to the beach
where cliffs provide shade

Swimming together
in paradise again
Laughing and jumping
in wonder with beloved

Water within/without
Sky and sea merge
We do as well
A couple of crazy kids

Walking back to Salema
We stop in the shade
for a tender embrace
Figueira return

8 – 17 October 2016

Shifting into higher gears
way beyond numbers
Connecting with Knowing
way beyond words

Seeing without pain
difficulties stretched back
to mother, grandmother
That Grandpa died alone

He had a heart attack
at only age fifty six
Life suddenly cut off
Wanted to teach me Yiddish

Joked on phone with kids
We'd visit second-hand shop
with potbellied stove
emitting warmth of love

I continue your potential
Mom, Grandma's too
Compassion beyond pain
turning *tsuris* into growth

*   *   *

Salema in my heart
wide as its bay
Safe harbour for boats
tractor pulls up

Quiet roar of waves
rolling onto beach
Now at low tide
allowing expanse

Sun through clouds
warming this body
Reflecting on waters
Salema in my heart

21 October 2016

Coming together as Autumn
as season changes do
Not exactly as I'd expected
but with much beauty

Splendour of yellows, reds
Leaves on trees and ground
Nourishing the Earth
I receive the bounty

Difficulties arise as well
leading to new possibilities
The car repaired to carry on
after not starting for Sangha sit

Meditated here with Bob instead
as we'd done in Salema
Our special love connection
magnified by mind-focus

Loved-one gradually improves
though needs hospitalisation
Told doctor that when better
wants to return to own flat

Good to be back at home
Grandkids coming for half term
Girls have such strong bond
Glad they're both doing well

Bob is painting in studio
inspired by Salema landscapes
Here I sit typing in study
Transformation emerges

Yes, there's sadness too
but that's aspect of the mix
As older friend with pain said
'It's only a small part of my life'

31 October – 6 November

Still morning fog hue
reflects tired body
A chance to lie down
release toward the Knowing

Back two weeks now
Had so much to do
Wonder of granddaughters
Reiki clients, teaching

Great to have lazy day
Meet Rahelly for tea
This morning is mine
to just be still, rest

*   *   *

Did I see anything special
Bob asks of my walk
No, but oh yes, I did
Such beauty and wonder

Saw the winding river
Gentle ripple of waters
Twenty-five swans upon her
Reunited for the winter

Houseboats moored on bank
Neighbours known for years
New ones come and go
as do thoughts and feelings

Staying with the positive
So much good fortune
Kevin gets Internship
extending paid PhD

Loved-one improves slowly
Had good talk with her OT
I've picked my first poem
for new book collection

8 November 2016

Sunny kitchen tea
Meditation of stopping
Sitting after breakfast
Breathing with tick tock clock

A chance to let go
Appreciate my life's beauty
Simply being with clean dishes
Plants on window sill

Holding up tea cup
Steamy fennel aroma
Feeling liquid warmth
Tongue, throat then belly

Synchronising with water
flowing in and out
Reconnecting as one
from rain to my body

Yes, I want to be here
rather than in worry
Loved-one sorrow
I grow from the sadness

Power of the sun
Eyes feel the gleam
Body so grateful
Frost burning away

With chill upon us
US election date
Loved-one in hospital
Brexit looming

I choose this vision
Way of seeing positive
reality of my life
Sunny kitchen tea

9 - 10 November 2016

Unbelievable Trump victory
I can only keep practicing
Knowing that's best way
from my previous experience

Love still trumps hate
whatever US result
Earth remains under feet
Solid as I breathe

Beauty still on Green
Nature's autumn show
undaunted by elections
In circular flow

As the river goes
back to sea again
Process and change
Unsure how will happen

What else can I do
but be with this instant
As church bells chime
I stop, take in freshness

From here best to cope
with what future brings
Shocking, disappointing
Love still trumps hate

*   *   *

Beauty and suffering
Seeing them both
Manifesting this moment
as Trump consequences sink in

Want to keep in proportion
while accepting sadness too
Mourning and organising
Knowing beauty and suffering

11 – 13 November 2016

Back to Nirvana
here all along
Open, unconditioned
Ultimate of pure Knowing

In difficult times
deepening's the way
into the beyond
from right here breathing

Seeing past to clear vision
Not caught in tangled despair
Being Reiki, giving treatment
Experiencing vibration

*   *   *

Needing time to rest
Come down into feelings
So heavy in chest
Numbness of mind

Slowly sipping tea
Nothing to do
Laying in conservatory
Listening to the rain

When it lets up
I venture forth on bike
Riding out to countryside
Peddling and Peddling

Coming back to draw
lines, shapes and colours
Not needing to be nice
Scribble scrabble galore

Before going to bed
Bob and I meditate
So grateful for our love
which will see us through

14 – 15 November 2016

Nirvana in Samsara
only place to find
that wondrous grace
is in my daily life

What looks like difficulty
is heart opening chance
Interwoven connections
past blinding notions

Beyond separation
is reality vision
where beauty's so vivid
with veil of fear lifting

In the naked Knowing
love can flow naturally
I want to open to you
to grow that wide and true

There I can see
past centuries of pain
to ease of vast being
Returning to wholeness

*   *   *

Nirvana Sun break
after days of whiteness
Lifting as I walk
to height of sky blue

Being with the energy
of river and earth
under feet, flowing through
Breathing in the light

Yes, so much better
than lost in despair
Only in Samsara
can I find Nirvana

Back to boundless love
in and out I go
Still return is sweet
Childhood feel again

Want it good for all
Energy remembered
Flowing in once more
as I open to it

Meditating with Sangha
Discourse On Love
Hearing in my heart
widening to the beauty

As when very young
holding onto buggy
Told my dear Aunt Ruty
Don't worry, it'll be OK

*   *   *

Wondrous mindful teaching
with advanced Reiki students
A day to return to energy
and to share our insights

Just what I needed
weighed down with fear, sadness
New US President
such a step backward

Returning to seeing
what I can change and not
Mind's only place to start
Perceptions emanate from there

So much more effective
Helping loved-ones, myself
and working for justice
Choosing happiness again

Rereading poems
for new collection
Drugging up pain
Awakened in the night

What can I do
but see you are there
Heartbreak reopened
Loved-one's past problems

Just want to let go
of worry and fear
Relearning lessons
but harder right now

With Loved-one in hospital
I especially need balance
to do what I can
without getting caught

Beyond grasping/aversion
is Middle Way, Thay says
Yes, I know it well
when return to Bodhicitta

Mind of love for me
where I have to start
with body scan, awareness
Good I noticed again

And what do poems say
but how I worked it out
Over and again
Heart breaks open

30 November - 3 December 2016

Concrete is poured
on neighbour's front garden
which adjoins ours

They concreted back one over
Now they want space to park
their second car in the front

Sorry, dear Mother Earth
We'll keep our land open
so you and children can breathe

That's the best I can do
Tried talking to neighbours
But don't want weeds or garden

As roar of giant mixer lorry
vibrates through the house
I choose nature's beauty

*   *   *

Being Bodhisattva
that I already am
Starting with myself
Focus, healing, nurturing

Breathing through pain
sadness, tangles galore
Methodically dealing with
the ones that I can

Enjoying sun beauty
for Joy and Loved-one
She smiled and danced after
stepped out of ward first time

Standing with Women in Black
Bundled in Market Square for Peace
Starting with energy for myself
allowing it to grow, ripple out

Embracing pain with compassion
Releasing to Earth through feet
In Tai Chi posture, letting go
Seeing grey sky above stalls

Birds glide across in beauty
Shoppers stop, read our signs
Mine says 'Scrap Trident
Fund Human Needs'

Some nod, smile back at me
Others ignore or just stare
Being with sisters, Reiki energy
available to all who want

Oh, so very healing
being a part of stream
of those standing for peace
over thousands of years

Swaying as Chi comes through
Some people even take leaflet
Then older man comes up to argue
Wanting us to say Israel racist, fascist

Liz explains vigils started in Israel
protesting Palestinian occupation
But his anger is way beyond reason
I'm caught, reply two of us are Jewish

Suddenly my focus is gone
feeling his anger wave hit
Not responding, but still I'm shaken
Then say, 'We're standing for Peace'

243

15 December 2016

FOR MICHELE THOMAS

We continue for you, dear Michele
with all the books and grace
Beauty of your warm charm
So welcoming and supportive

From the time when we met
through First Feminist Book Week
You selling the volumes
at Women's Centre events

So encouraging, Michele
I could feel it inside
Not yet a published writer
but you believed in us all

Yes, we could do it
New generations rediscovering
women's words, lives anew
You restocking on the shelves

Advice on Women's Studies
when I worked on that text
'And, of course, we shall have
the book launch at Heffers'

So pleased for your friendship
cordial dinners and chats
So many connections
France, the States, ex-pats

Always so glad to see us
Encouraging writers' muse
Telling of books read
So a part of that world

We carry on with your spirit
The energy flows through us
still holding hands and smiling
We continue for you, dear Michele

16 December 2016

Coming back up once more
after another bad night's sleep
Working with preoccupations
Sadness about Loved-one

Over so many years
you've been my Life Koan
Thay says made stronger
each time can transform

Compassion for you
Such a difficult life
though happiness, too
in your own way

Nurse says you're calmer
when I'm around
Can only contribute that
if I build it inside

Anchoring and breathing
Not to wander off to despair
I hold you in tender circle
of kind understanding

Many years they didn't recognise
Autistic Spectrum Disorder
So we did the best we could
and just kept on loving you

Reading poems not easy
brings back such hard times
And these aren't easy either
Brexit, Trump, you in hospital

But also poems of wonder
Granddaughters and family
Thrill of nature on Common
Coming back up once more

CHANUKAH AND NEW YEAR

Chanukah Together
Warm family tradition
Girls so big now
lighting the *menorah*

Helena says remembers
Sophie lifted up to candles
Ella just a baby then
Both fascinated by flame

After so many years
I say she's honorary Jew
Helena happily accepts
We prepare *dreidel* game

Sophie gets new smart phone
Puts on apps to communicate
and she's off and running
Already knows more than me

Ella's new Electric Guitar
plays us what she knows
Wants folk music too
We sing This Land Is Your Land

Sophie reads her old writings
I've kept for her in binder
Brings back her long link
to her special creative knack

Ella says can she come
on Plum Village retreat
I ask Sophie about going
She answers definitely, 'Yes'

So we'll go with Kevin too
Much adventure, transformation
We all make cards for Loved-one
I'll bring to her in hospital

Bob's special cards from paintings
They each pick one to take home
We send them out to friends, family
For a Happy New Year

*   *   *

Shoyn tsite freiheit
It's about time Freedom
What am I waiting for
Only I can do it

All the way you look at things
I need to keep coming back
to seeing the beauty
Being Nirvana

Only from that perspective
Can the insight shine through
To hell with these ruts
of negative blocks

With new year approaching
Need the resolution
of farsighted vision
to breakthrough to clarity

It's not about fighting
but just letting go
Sometimes you just need
to have had enough of it

I know the direction
where I want to step forward
And how to get there
It's just trusting Joy to do it

Not trying so hard
or caring too much
Just resonating with True Nature
Shoyn tsite freiheit

4 – 7 January 2017

Picking poems and editing
Two volumes already published
energy flows into now

Yellow light of faith
Not blind but based
on my own experience

All I need do is let go
of worry and grasping
Fear of the unknown

Being the trust and confidence
Reconnecting 'done it before'
True loyalty spins this way

*   *   *

Ask ancestors to be protectors
both spiritual and biological
At New Year's ceremony
in Phouc and Phung temple

Protecting my mind
before, during and after
hospital visit with Loved-one
Intent to offer peace, happiness

Wanting clarity, stability
trusting Store Consciousness
Doing what I can
in complex situation

Offering my presence
support and suggestions
Being with my daughter
Preparing her daughter's visit

Then meeting Kev at station
His vision so reassuring
Helping to bring me back
to seeing long term positive

Trusting his perspective
and Store from experience
knowing, building from practice
Ask ancestors to be protectors

*   *   *

Amethyst Crystals clearing
back to original nature
Resonating comfort
Value of family love

Birthstone of grandmother
mother, Ella and I
And there's the necklace
warn by Mom, Grandma

Passed down to me
but too heavy to wear
Took off three stones
Macramed to new necklace

Rest of stones awaiting
opportunity to continue
Gave to children too young
Try again for them, grandkids

Not cleansing the necklace
but leaving original energy
of Grandma Rose and Florence
sending maternal love

8 –15 January 2017

Slipping back into Nirvana
Oh, so very needed
that I come into memory
Returning with release

Becoming available
to sea gulls, vast sky
Bare branches, wide bark
Into place of seeing, being

How many walks, poems
of this very experience
help me to revisit
Slipping back into Nirvana

*   *   *

Embracing a mother's heavy heart
with Tai Chi, porridge and love
Held in Bodhicitta mind
where it can heal and rest

Letting the peace penetrate
into the sadness, gloom
Just sitting here breathing with it
Embracing a mother's heavy heart

*   *   *

17 January 2017

Red streaked sunset
bringing perspective
on ride back from visit
to Loved-one in hospital

Yes, improvement
though slow, uneven
But walked down corridor
with me to Family Room

First time she's done that
preparing for daughter's visit
So wants to see her
willing to step out further

Writing more in book
as well as drawing
We meet with team
about going back to flat

She's not ready to do so yet
and doctor's still honing meds
But says progress being made
so her daughter can come

247

18 January 2017

We Shall Overcome again
Singing, playing on guitar
Bob bought us for reconnection
to musical spirit of our youth

Needed for Trump's inauguration
Brexit, clearly going to happen
Bridges Not Walls, as Dr King said
We'll drape the Elizabeth Way one

With banners through time
touching old persevering energy
Connecting with new generations
Uplifting so deep in heart

Like Civil Rights Movement
Holding hands, arms crossed
Swaying, singing together
Feeding harmony, hope actions

As teen in Newark
wouldn't have imagined
future here in Britain
or need for song now

But that's the reality
as Mom would say
So energy rises forth
We Shall Overcome again

20 January 2017

Trump inauguration
Brexit firmness
We stand against the tide
Holding hands worldwide

Singing We Shall Overcome
on sunlit bridge
wrapped with Banners
for justice and peace

With our hands and voices
building hope, inspiration
In time of despondency
returning to creative acts

Kevin at US Embassy
Helena to Women's March
with IMELDA sisters
Performance protest

Ella's drawing sign
she'll join her mum later
with Kev as a family
Fannie would be pleased

We celebrate her birthday
as she would have wanted
Keep on demonstrating
using resourceful skills

So I come back again
to transformation energy
Embracing despair
Singing We Shall Overcome

22 January 2017

Hope bursts forth
through Women's Marches
Half million in Washington
Three million throughout States

Worldwide they pack streets
Pink hated women
and their male supporters
In vast peaceful protests

Ninety thousand in London
Ella, Kev, Helena there
Ella, schoolmates lead chants
striding out with diversity

Old and new generations
just had to come and join
to show their opposition
International solidarity

Helena's IMELDA group
perform for abortion rights
in Ireland, North and South
US and everywhere

Amazing cultural shift
So many young women
Newcomers to demos
Plethora of hand-made signs

'I won't go quietly
back to the 1950s'
Coat hanger with words
'Never Again'

Not just the usual suspects
but mass arising of spirit
After march, artistic signs attached
to fence round National Gallery

So fresh energy surfaces
To defend women's rights
migrants and minorities
All coming together

Speakers tell diverse crowd
'This is upside of downside'
'Our inclusive feminism
chooses love not hate'

'No human being is illegal'
'We are collective agents
of history, can't be deleted'
'United for body integrity'

Co-organiser wearing headscarf
tells oceans of campaigners
that she is her Palestinian
grandmother's wildest dream

Back in San Francisco
Joan Baez sings in Spanish
We Shall Not be Moved
I sing along in Britain

Immersed in sea of people's
collective consciousness
lifting all our spirits
Hope bursts forth

29 – 30 January 2017

The spirit of love unity
is greater than difficulties
Surpassing them yesterday
daughter and hers meet

In hospital Family Room
they are reunited
Hug, talk and draw
We sweetly sing

Feels like I moved heaven, earth
to make reconnection possible
Milestone for Loved-one
Kindness of her daughter

A blessing for us all
May we each reap the fruits
Growing into our potentials
such possible opportunities

*   *   *

Hopeless to control future
Better stick to Now
Shock realisation
been trying to fix chaos

But chaos is the nature
of effortless life flow
beyond my need for order
security, improvement

Seeing brought me back
to vividness of Green
Contrast of grass, dried leaves
Multi-textured bark

Pack of swans grazing
upon shore of river
gently rippling own way
Hopeless to control

18 February 2017

Postponing Publication
Taking back my life
to create best book
Not under such pressure
to edit, edit, carry on

Thought date realistic
but turns out it's not
Better to realise, reschedule
Insight comes to me in night
seeing I'm under such stress

With book launch detached
from my turning 70
just want warm family birthday
Not driving me morn to evening
into haze to get book done

Want a chance to settle
back into normal life
Working at slower pace
with more clarity of vision
Enjoying it more

Out on the Green
I notice what's below
Fear Loved-one'll be so needy
that book won't get finished
or more distractions from party

So celebrating turning 70
combined with book launch
moves further from birthday
But when conditions are right
it'll take it's course and happen

Returning to stiller state
Preparing to visit Loved-one
talk to doctor of autism
Bringing all the old papers
hoping realistic diagnosis

Bulbs start to rise up
I discover clearing brush
Still working on poems
but not editing under pressure

First Daffodil blossoms
unfurling toward spring
I need to do the same
Not possible if body fails

Putting so much pressure
based on misperception
that need book out sooner
Things'll only get worse

So I have to step back
give Loved-one and I space
though I hope for diagnosis
of Autistic Spectrum Disorder

Am preparing presentation
But to do the best I can
Need awareness of own needs
Take good care of Joy

*   *   *

Nirvana breaks through
Sure, all hell's breaking loose
Ying and yang both there
I choose timeless Now

In this instant of birdsong
sweetness penetrates so deeply
I see puddle reflecting
bare branches, white sky

Here with Mother Nature
as Mom used to call it
we resonate the beauty
of snowdrops out again

*   *   *

Back with the guitar
old friend from teens
Reconnected last months
after Bob bought for us

Hootenannying alone
old favourites and new
Cords coming back
The wonder of singing

Adding Plum Village songs
that can play with simple cords
Amazing how they're building up
Great focus and release

Practice in the evenings
before meditating with Bob
Together so healing
Raising my spirits

Returning, see how I missed
being one-woman band
Voice opening's so freeing
Back with the guitar

27 February 2017

Finally a real diagnosis
of High Functioning Autism
written down by consult
Not just me saying it

I've gone on for so long
trying to get them to see
Showing Loved-one's old reports
Explaining her difficulties

After all this time
not only am I vindicated
But much more importantly
She can get the right help

Consultant says he'll work with her
to get back language memory skills
He's impressed by her intelligence
and they'll get her to be alright

Psychologist says it's evident
She'll also work with Loved-one
Such a relief to leave them to it
and enjoy upcoming birthday

5 March 2017

Asperger Syndrome
Clarified diagnosis
Can hardly believe it
after years of saying that
Reading, seeing it so clearly

Why couldn't it come earlier
13 years ago when tested
Male oriented, ridged then
Now conditions are right
Best not stuck in Second Arrow

This time she'll have support
Med changes, one not needed
but Loved-one's been taking
for years clouding her mind
in yet more confusion

Fresh start, as with spring
We post her affirmations
on hospital room wall
'I feel happy, safe, peaceful'
May these energies bloom in her

7 March 2017

Releasing to Seventy
in family surround
Special time together
beyond expectations

Cake, cards, food
all handmade
Contributing to warmth
Love of our life stream

Satisfied, relieved
taking in joyful vibes
Happiness, caring
each expressed in own way

Singing old folk songs
Me and Ella on guitars
Voices join harmoniously
back to when I was 18

Ella asks about me then
What I'd think of me now
Young Joy'd be surprised
but it turned out well

Sophie fascinated
I explain about activism
Sing Civil Rights songs
Now we all go on demos

Feel continuation
link to forgotten Joy
So healing for all ages
Taking in family love

So helpful old dark cloud
surrounding Loved-one's
long misunderstandings
slowly lifting with diagnosis

Close friends send cards
Support, good wishes
Sue surprises with gift
Kev's pottery tree expanse

Ella, Kev stay for weekend
Their energy contagious
building ours with closeness
intergenerational beauty

On the Green this morning
Awareness vivid with sun
that not much more time
Do want to use it wisely

ELLA'S DOG AND SOPHIE'S TRAVELS

From when very young
Ella's wanted a dog
Parents said when old enough
to take care of it, could get one

'How old is that', she asked
They picked the age of 11
So very far away
starting secondary school

As the years passed
Ella never changed her mind
They live in a small flat
So would get a small dog

Growing up she researched
different dogs, crossbreeds
Asked to pet passing ones
find out what kind they were

What is a friendly type
likes to be with children
Miniature poodle and
various variations

Suddenly the day came
when Ella turned 11
Parents out looking
for right family dog

Enter Jaffa, rescue dog
abandoned in Cyprus
Told she was right match
Flown into their lives

Ella incredibly excited
picked her up with Kevin
Small, fluffy, shaking
Ella held her on lap

Dog began to settle in
Ella's been in heaven
Her dream come true
Sweet affectionate Jaffa

Perhaps we all need
that fluffy love within us
Kev, Helena taken to her
Ella, Jaffa found each other

*　　　*　　　*

Sophie taking trains
London, back herself
So grown up, capable
Coming into own power

Yesterday writing story
Great she has the outlet
talent, perseverance
to express herself that way

Today off to spend weekend
with Ella, Helena, Kevin
Him meeting at Kings Cross
after I put her on the train

Her independence blooming
coming back round to confidence
That old sense of herself
New variations as teen

So connected to London family
them always glad to have her
Showing their dog, Jaffa
Picking Ella up at acting class

And we can just enjoy
their happiness together
Special time of their visit
Sophie flourishing in own way

20 March 2017

Stepping out to Nirvana
beyond preconceptions
Just seeing the grass
dried leaves dance across

Wind blowing through
I go in your direction
Being with your force
Spotted dog wags tail

And I am just here
walking upon Mother
In tune with gravity
easily sinking down

Wind calms as I reach river
Face freshened by drizzle
rejoining rolling ripples
heading back to the sea

Releasing concerns
heart softens wider
Beyond the grip
such beauty appears

Feed me, I need it
Speckle of bark
of London Plane Tree
brown hues wonder

Branches in three dimension
reaching out toward growth
I do the same
in this very instant

Wind up again
I welcome it's cleansing
Blow away my worries
so I can be free

Rain upon my hood
as I head back home
Bob asks where I've been
Stepping out in Nirvana

www.ingramcontent.com/pod-product-compliance
Lightning Source LLC
Chambersburg PA
CBHW072341090426
42741CB00012B/2874